THE OVERCOMING **LIFE**

*But be ye doers of the word, and not hearers only,
deceiving your own selves. – James 1:22*

D1509795

ANEKO
PRESS

We love hearing from our readers. Please contact us at www.anekopress.com/questions-comments with any questions, comments, or suggestions.

Cover Design: Natalia Hawthorne

Editors: Heather Thomas and Ruth Zetek

Printed in the United States of America

Aneko Press

www.anekopress.com

Aneko Press, Life Sentence Publishing, and our logos are trademarks of

Life Sentence Publishing, Inc.
203 E. Birch Street
P.O. Box 652
Abbotsford, WI 54405

RELIGION / Christian Life / Spiritual Growth

Paperback ISBN: 978-1-62245-386-3

eBook ISBN: 978-1-62245-387-0

10 9 8 7 6 5 4 3 2

Available where books are sold

Contents

PART I

The Christian's Warfare

For whatever is born of God overcomes the world; and this is the victory that has overcome the world -our faith. Who is the one who overcomes the world, but he who believes that Jesus is the Son of God? (1 John 5:4-5)

When a battle is fought, we are anxious to know who the victors are. In these verses, we are told who will gain the victory in life. When I was converted, I made a mistake. I thought the battle was already mine, the victory already won, and the crown already in my grasp. I thought the old things had passed away, and all things had become new. I incorrectly believed that my old, corrupt nature, the Adam life, was gone. However, I found out, after serving Christ for a few months, that conversion was only like enlisting in the army. There was a battle taking place and if I was to receive a crown, I had to work for it and fight for it.

Salvation is a gift, as free as the air we breathe. It is obtained like any other gift, without money and without price. There are no other terms. *But to the one who does not work, but believes in Him who justifies the ungodly, his faith is credited as righteousness* (Romans 4:5). But on the other hand, if we are to gain a crown, we must work for it. *For no man can lay a foundation other than the one which is laid, which is Jesus Christ. Now if any man builds on the foundation with gold, silver, precious stones, wood, hay, straw, each man's work will become evident; for the day will show it because it is to be revealed with fire, and the fire itself will test the quality of each man's work. If any man's work which he has built on it remains, he will receive a reward. If any man's work is burned up, he will suffer loss; but he himself will be saved, yet so as through fire* (1 Corinthians 3:11-15).

Enlisting is one thing and participating in a battle is quite another.

We see clearly from this that it is possible to be saved, and all our works burned up. It's possible for us to have a wretched, miserable voyage through life, with no victory, and no reward at the end. I am saved, yet as by fire, or as Job puts it, *by the skin of my teeth* (Job 19:20). I believe a great many men will barely get to heaven, just as Lot escaped Sodom. They will be burned out with nothing left. Their works and everything else will be destroyed.

When a man enters the army, he's a member of the army the moment he enlists. However, he is just as much a member as a man who has been in the army ten or twenty years. But enlisting is one thing and participating in a battle is quite another. Young converts are like those who just enlisted.

It's foolish for any man to attempt to fight in his own

strength. The world, the flesh, and the Devil are too much for any man. We will gain the victory over every enemy if we are linked to Christ by faith, and He is steadily formed in us. It is believers who are the overcomers. *But thanks be to God, who always leads us in triumph in Christ, and manifests through us the sweet aroma of the knowledge of Him in every place* (2 Corinthians 2:14). Through Him, we will be more than conquerors.

I wouldn't even think of talking to unconverted men about overcoming the world, for it's utterly impossible for them to do so. They might as well try to cut down the American forest with their pocketknives. Unfortunately, many Christian people make the mistake of thinking that the battle is already fought and won. They believe that all they have to do is put the oars down in the bottom of the boat, and the current will drift them into the ocean of God's eternal love. But we have to cross the current. We have to learn how to watch, fight, and overcome. The battle has only just begun. The Christian life is a conflict and warfare. The quicker we understand this reality the better. There isn't a blessing in this world that God hasn't linked Himself to. God associates Himself with all the great and higher blessings. When God and man work together, there will be victory. We are coworkers with Him. If you take a water-powered mill and put it forty feet above a river, there isn't enough money in the world to make that river turn the mill. Lower it about forty feet and away it works. We need to keep in mind that if we are going to overcome the world, we must work with God. It is His power that makes the way of grace possible.

The story is told that Frederick Douglass, the great

slave orator, once said in a mournful speech when things looked dark for his race, "The white man is against us, governments are against us, and the spirit of the times is against us. I see no hope for the colored race. I am full of sadness."

Just then, a poor, old, colored woman rose in the audience and said, "Frederick, is God dead?" My friend, it makes a difference when you count God in.

A young believer can often become discouraged and disheartened when he realizes this warfare. He begins to think that God has forsaken him, and that Christianity is not all that it claims to be. Instead, he should consider it an encouraging sign. No sooner has a soul escaped from his snare than the great adversary takes steps to ensnare it again. He utilizes all his power to recapture his lost prey. The fiercest attacks are made on the strongest forts. The fierce battles the young believer is called on to wage is the evidence of the work of the Holy Spirit in his heart. God will not desert him in his time of need any more than He deserted His people of old when they were hard-pressed by their foes.

The Only Complete Victor

You are from God, little children, and have overcome them; because greater is He who is in you than he who is in the world (1 John 4:4). The only man that ever conquered this world – as the complete victor – was Jesus Christ. When He shouted on the cross, *It is finished!* it was the shout of a conqueror. He had overcome every enemy. He had met sin and death. He had met every foe that you and I will ever meet, and came through as the victor. If I have the spirit of Christ, if I have that same life in me, then I have a power greater than any power in the world. It is with that same power I overcome the world.

Notice that everything human in this world fails. Every man, the moment he takes his eyes off God, fails. Every man has been a failure at some period of his life. Abraham failed. Moses failed. Elijah failed. Consider the men that have become so famous and were so mighty. The moment they took their eyes off God, they became weak like other men. It's a very strange thing that those men failed on the strongest point of their character. I suppose it was because they were not on guard. Abraham was noted for his faith, but laughed when God told him he and Sarah would have a child. Moses was noted for his meekness and humility, but he failed when he got angry. God kept him out of the Promised Land because he lost his temper. I know he was called the servant of God, and that he was a mighty man, and had power with God, but humanly speaking, he failed, and was kept out of the Promised Land. Elijah was noted for his power in prayer and for his courage, yet he became a coward. He was the boldest man of his day. He stood before Ahab, the royal court, and all the prophets of Baal. Yet, when he heard that Jezebel had threatened his life, he ran away to the desert. Under a juniper tree, he prayed to die. Peter was noted for his boldness, and a little maid scared him nearly out of his wits. As soon as she spoke to him, he trembled and swore that he didn't know Christ. I have often said to myself that I'd like to have been there on the day of Pentecost, alongside that maid, when she saw Peter preach.

I suppose she said, "What has come over that man? He was afraid of *me* only a few weeks ago. Now he stands up before all Jerusalem and charges these very Jews with the murder of Jesus."

Triumphs of Faith

Now, how are we to get the victory over all our enemies? We live by faith. *I have been crucified with Christ; and it is no longer I who live, but Christ lives in me; and the life which I now live in the flesh I live by faith in the Son of God, who loved me and gave Himself up for me* (Galatians 2:20). We get this life by faith, and become linked to Immanuel – *God with us*. If I have God for me, I am going to overcome. How do we gain this mighty power? By faith.

The most immature Christians I know are those who want to walk by sight.

Quite right, they were broken off for their unbelief, but you stand by your faith (Romans 11:20a). The Jews were cut off on account of their unbelief. We were grafted in on account of our belief. We live by faith, and we stand by faith.

Next, we walk by faith. *For we walk by faith, not by sight* (2 Corinthians 5:7). The most immature Christians I know are those who want to walk by sight. They want to see how a thing is going to come out. That isn't walking by faith at all. That's walking by sight.

I think the people whose lives best represent this difference are Joseph and Jacob. Jacob was a man who walked with God by sight. You remember his vow at Bethel: *If God will be with me and will keep me on this journey that I take, and will give me food to eat and garments to wear, and I return to my father's house in safety, then the LORD will be my God* (Genesis 28:20-21). Remember how his heart revived when he saw the wagons Joseph sent him from Egypt? He sought after signs. He never could have gone through the temptations and trials that his son Joseph did. Joseph represents a more mature Christian. He could walk in the dark. He survived thirteen years of misfortune, in spite of his dreams, and then credited it all to the goodness and providence of God.

Lot and Abraham are also a good illustration. Lot turned away from Abraham and tented on the plains of Sodom. He claimed a good stretch of pastureland but had bad neighbors. He had a weak character and should have stayed with Abraham in order to get strong. Many men are just like that. As long as their mothers are living, or they're shored up by some other godly person, they get along fine. But they can't stand alone. Lot walked by sight. But Abraham walked by faith and walked in the footsteps ordained by God. *By faith Abraham, when he was called, obeyed by going out to a place which he was to receive for an inheritance; and he went out, not knowing where he was going. By faith he lived as an alien in the land of promise, as in a foreign land, dwelling in tents with Isaac and Jacob, fellow heirs of the same promise; for he was looking for the city which has foundations, whose architect and builder is God* (Hebrews 11:8-10).

Finally, we fight by faith. *In addition to all, taking up*

the shield of faith with which you will be able to extinguish all the flaming arrows of the evil one (Ephesians 6:16). Every dart Satan fires at us can be quenched by faith. By faith, we can overcome the Evil One. To fear is to have more faith in your antagonist than in Christ.

In the very early days of the Civil War, Secretary Seward, who was Lincoln's Secretary of State and a shrewd politician, prophesied that the war would be over in ninety days. Young men in thousands and hundreds of thousands came forward and volunteered to go down to Dixie and whip the South. They thought they would be back in ninety days. The war lasted four years and cost about half a million lives. What was the matter? The South was a good deal stronger than the North assumed. Its strength was underestimated.

Jesus Christ makes no mistake of that kind. When He enlists a man in His service, He shows him the dark side. He lets him know that he must live a life of self-denial. If a man is not willing to go to heaven by the way of Calvary, he cannot go at all. Many men want a religion in which there is no cross, but they cannot enter heaven that way. If we are to be disciples of Jesus Christ, we must deny ourselves and take up our cross and follow Him. So let's sit down and count the cost. Don't think that you will have no battles if you follow the Nazarene, because many battles are before you. Yet if I had ten thousand lives, Jesus Christ would have every one of them. Men do not object to a battle if they are confident they will achieve victory. Praise God, victory is possible for all of us.

The reason so many Christians fail all through life is

that they underestimate the strength of the Enemy. We have a terrible Enemy to contend with. Don't let Satan deceive you. Unless you are spiritually dead, it means warfare. Nearly everything around us tends to draw us away from God. We don't step straight from Egypt to the throne of God. There's the wilderness journey and there are enemies in the land.

Don't let any man or woman think that all he or she has to do is join the church. That will not save you. The question is, are you overcoming the world, or is the world overcoming you? Are you more patient than you were five years ago? Are you more good-natured? If you are not, the world is overcoming you, even if you are a church member. The epistle Paul

The question is, are you overcoming the world, or is the world overcoming you?

wrote to Titus says that we are to be *sound in faith, in charity, in tolerance*. We've got Christians, a good many of them, that walk victoriously in some areas but are immature in others. From outward appearances, just a piece of them seems to be saved. They aren't rounded out in their characters. It's just because they haven't been taught that they have a terrible foe to overcome.

If I wanted to find out whether a man was a Christian, I wouldn't go to his minister. I would go and ask his wife. We need more Christian life at home. If a man doesn't treat his wife right, I don't want to hear him talk about Christianity. What's the use of his talking about salvation for the next life, if he has no salvation for this one? We want a Christianity that goes into our homes and everyday lives. Some men's religion just repels me. They put on a whining voice, a sort of religious tone, and talk so sanctimoniously on Sunday that you would think they were wonderful saints. Then on Monday they are quite different. They put their religion away with their clothes, and you don't see any more of it until the next Sunday. You laugh, but let's be careful that we don't belong to that group. We must possess a more mature Christianity, or the church is gone. It's wrong for a man or woman to profess what they don't possess. If you are not overcoming temptations, the world is overcoming you. Just get on your knees and ask God to help you. Let us go to God, and ask Him to search us. Let's ask Him to wake us up and not think that just because we are church members we are all right. We are all wrong if we aren't achieving victory over sin.

PART II

Internal Foes

Now if we are going to overcome, we must begin inside. God always begins there. An enemy inside the fort is far more dangerous than one outside.

Scripture teaches that in every believer there are two natures warring against each other. *For we know that the Law is spiritual, but I am of flesh, sold into bondage to sin. For what I am doing, I do not understand; for I am not practicing what I would like to do, but I am doing the very thing I hate. But if I do the very thing I do not want to do, I agree with the Law, confessing that the Law is good. So now, no longer am I the one doing it, but sin which dwells in me. For I know that nothing good dwells in me, that is, in my flesh; for the willing is present in me, but the doing of the good is not. For the good that I want, I do not do, but I practice the very evil that I do not want. But if I am doing the very thing I do not want, I am no longer the one doing it, but sin which dwells in me. I find then the principle that evil is present in me, the one who wants to do good. For I joyfully concur with the law of God in the inner man, but I see a different law in the members of my body, waging war against the law of my mind and making me a prisoner of the law of sin which is in my members* (Romans 7:14-23). Again, in the epistle to the Galatians, he says, *For the flesh sets its desire against the Spirit, and the Spirit against the flesh; for these are in opposition to one another, so that you may not do the things that you please* (Galatians 5:17).

When we are born of God, we get His nature, but He does not immediately take away all the old nature. Each species of animal and bird is true to its nature. You can tell the nature of the dove or canary. The horse is true to its nature, and the cow is true to hers. But a man has two natures. Do not let the world or Satan make you think that the old nature is extinct, because it is not. *Even so consider yourselves to be dead to sin, but alive to God in Christ Jesus* (Romans 6:11). If you *were* dead, you wouldn't need to reckon yourselves dead, would you? The dead self would be dropped out of the reckoning. Then Paul states in 1 Corinthians 9:27 (JUB): *I keep my body under.* If it were dead, Paul wouldn't have needed to keep it under. I am judicially dead, but the old nature is alive. Therefore, if I don't keep my body under and crucify the flesh with its affections, this lower nature will gain the advantage, and I will be in bondage. Many men live all their lives in bondage to the old nature, when they could have liberty if they would only live the overcoming life. The old Adam never dies. It remains corrupt. *From the sole of the foot even to the head there is nothing sound in it, only bruises, welts and raw wounds, not pressed out or bandaged, nor softened with oil* (Isaiah 1:6).

A gentleman in India once got a tiger cub and tamed it so that it became a pet. One day when it had grown up, it tasted blood. The old tiger-nature flashed out, and it had to be killed. *"I" is the center of S-I-N.* It's the same with the old nature in the believer. It never dies, though it is subdued. Unless he is watchful and prayerful, the old nature will gain the upper hand and rush him into sin. Someone once pointed out that "I" is the center of S-I-N. It's the instrument through which Satan acts. The worst enemy you have to overcome, after all, is *yourself.*

When Capt. T. became converted in London, he was a great society man. After he had been a Christian some months, he was asked, "What have you found to be your greatest enemy since you became a Christian?"

After a few minutes of deep thought he said, "Well, I think it is myself."

"Ah!" said the lady. "The King has taken you into His presence, for it is only in His presence that we are taught these truths."

I have had more trouble with D. L. Moody than with any other man who has crossed my path. If I can keep him right, I don't have any trouble with other people. Many people have trouble with employees. Did you ever think that the trouble lies with you instead of the employee? Or if one member of the family is constantly snapping, he will have the whole family snapping. It's true whether you believe it or not. You speak quickly and snappishly to people and they will do the same to you.

Appetite

Now take *appetite*. That is an enemy inside. How many young men are ruined by the appetite for strong drink. Many have grown up to be a curse to their father and mother instead of a blessing. Not long ago, the body of a young suicide victim was discovered in one of our large cities. In his pocket was found a paper on which he had written, "I have done this myself. Don't tell anyone. It's all through drink." A hint of these facts in the public press drew 246 letters from 246 families, each of whom had a prodigal son who, it was feared, might be the suicide.

Strong drink is an enemy, both to body and soul. It is reported that Sir Andrew Clarke, the celebrated London physician, once made the following statement: "Now let me say that I am speaking solemnly and carefully when I tell you that I am considerably within the mark in saying that within the rounds of my hospital wards today, seven out of every ten that lie there in their beds owe their ill health to alcohol. I do not say that seventy in every hundred are drunkards; I do not know that one of them is; but they use alcohol. So soon as a man begins to take one drop, then the desire begotten in him becomes a part of his nature, and that nature, formed by his acts, inflicts curses inexpressible when handed down to the generations that aspire to follow him as part and parcel of their being. When I think of this I am disposed to give up my profession—to give up everything—and go forth upon a holy crusade to preach to all men, 'Beware of this enemy of the race!'"

It is the most destructive force in the world today. It kills more than the bloodiest wars. It is the fruitful parent of crime, idleness, poverty, and disease. It spoils a man for this world and damns him for the next. The Word of God has declared it: *Or do you not know that the unrighteous will not inherit the kingdom of God? Do not be deceived; neither fornicators, nor idolaters, nor adulterers ... nor drunkards ... will inherit the kingdom of God* (1 Corinthians 6:9-10).

How can we overcome this enemy? Bitter experience proves that man is not powerful enough in his own strength. The only cure for the accursed appetite is regeneration – a new life – the power of the risen Christ within us. Let a man that is prone to strong drink look to God for help, and He will give him victory over his appetite. Jesus Christ came to destroy the works of the Devil, and He will take away that appetite if you will let Him.

Temper

Then there is *temper*. I wouldn't give much for a man that doesn't have a temper. Steel isn't good for anything if it hasn't got temper. But when temper gets the mastery over me, I am its slave, and it becomes a source of weakness. It may be made a great power for good all through my life and help me. Or it may become my greatest enemy from within and rob me of power. The current in some rivers is so strong that it makes them useless for navigation.

Someone said that a preacher will never fail to reach

the people when he speaks of temper. It is astonishing how little mastery even professing Christians have over it. A friend of mine in England visited a certain home. While he sat in the parlor, he heard a noise in the hall. He asked what it was and was told that it was only the doctor throwing his boots downstairs because they weren't properly polished. "Many Christians," said an old clergyman, "who bore the loss of a child or of all their property with the most heroic Christian fortitude are entirely vanquished by the breaking of a dish or the blunders of a servant."

I have had people say to me, "Mr. Moody, how can I get control of my temper?"

If you really want to get control, I will tell you how. But you won't like the medicine. Treat it as a sin and confess it. People look upon it as a sort of affliction. One lady even told me she inherited it from her father and mother. I suppose she did. That is still no excuse for her.

When you get angry next time and speak unkindly to a person and realize it, go and ask that person to forgive you. You won't get mad with that person for the next twenty-four hours. You might do it in about forty-eight hours, but go the second time. After you've done that about half a dozen times, you'll change your behavior, because apologizing makes the old flesh burn.

A lady said to me once, "I have gotten so in the habit of exaggerating that my friends accuse me of exaggerating so much that they don't believe me."

She said, "Can you help me? What can I do to overcome it?"

"Well," I said, "the next time you catch yourself lying, go right to that party and say you have lied, and tell them you're sorry. Say it is a lie. Stamp it out, root and branch. That's what you want to do."

"Oh," she said, "I wouldn't like to call it *lying*." But that is what it was.

Christianity isn't worth a snap of your finger if it doesn't straighten out your character. I've grown tired of all mere lip service and sentiment. If people can't tell when you are telling the truth, there is something radically wrong, and you had better straighten it out right away. Now, are you ready to *do* it? Bring yourself to the point of dealing with it

Confession never fails to bring a blessing.

whether you want to or not. Do you know someone who has been offended by something you've done? Go right to them and tell them you are sorry. You say you are not to blame. Never mind, go right to them and tell them you are sorry. I have had to do it many times. An impulsive man like myself has to do it often, but I sleep all the sweeter at night when I get things straightened out. Confession never fails to bring a blessing. I have sometimes had to get off the platform and go down to ask a man's forgiveness before I could continue preaching. A Christian man ought to be a gentleman every time. If he is not, and he finds he has wounded or hurt someone, he ought to go and straighten it out at once. There are many people who want just enough Christianity to make them respectable. They don't think about this overcoming life that gets the victory all the time. They have their blue days and their angry days, and the children say, "Mother is in a bad mood today. You will have to be very careful."

We don't want any of those touchy blue days with their ups and downs. If we are overcoming, others will have confidence in our Christianity. The reason many men have no power is that there is some cursed sin covered up. There will not be a drop of dew until that sin is brought to light. Get right inside. We can go out like giants and conquer the world if everything is right within.

Paul says that we are to be sound in faith, in patience, and in love. If a man is unsound in his faith, the clergy takes the ecclesiastical sword and cuts him off immediately. However, if he is unsound in love or patience, nothing is said about that. We must be sound in faith, in love, and in patience if we are to be true to God.

How delightful it is to meet a man who can control his temper. It is said of Wilberforce that a friend once found him in great agitation, looking for a dispatch he had misplaced for which one of the royal family was waiting. Just then, as if to make it even more trying, a disturbance was heard in the nursery.

"Now," thought the friend, "surely his temper will give way."

The thought had hardly passed through his mind when Wilberforce turned to him and said, "What a blessing it is to hear those dear children. Only think what a relief, among other hurries, to hear their voices and know they are well."

Covetousness

Take the sin of *covetousness*. There is more said in the Bible against it than against drunkenness. I must get it out of me – destroy it, root and branch – and not let it have dominion over me. We think that a man who gets drunk is a horrid monster, but a covetous man will often be received into the church and put into office, who is as vile and black in the sight of God as any drunkard.

The most dangerous thing about this sin is that it is not generally regarded as horribly wicked. Of course, we all have contempt for those who hoard their wealth, but all covetous men are not misers. Another thing to be noted about covetousness is that the old are more prone to it than the young.

Let's see what the Bible says about covetousness:

> *Therefore consider the members of your earthly body as dead to immorality, impurity, passion, evil desire, and greed, which amounts to idolatry* (Colossians 3:5).

> *For this you know with certainty, that no immoral or impure person or covetous man, who is an idolater, has an inheritance in the kingdom of Christ and God* (Ephesians 5:5).

> *But those who want to get rich fall into temptation and a snare and many foolish and harmful desires which plunge men into ruin and destruction. For the love of money is a root of all sorts of evil, and some by longing for it have wandered away from the faith*

and pierced themselves with many griefs
(1 Timothy 6:9-10).

*For the wicked boasts of his heart's desire, and
the greedy man curses and spurns the LORD*
(Psalm 10:3).

Covetousness enticed Lot into Sodom. It caused the destruction of Achan and all his house. It was the iniquity of Balaam. It was the sin of Samuel's sons. It left Gehazi a leper. It sent the rich young ruler away sorrowful. It led Judas to sell his Master and Lord for thirty pieces of silver. It brought about the death of Ananias and Sapphira. It was the blot in the character of Felix. What victims it has had in all ages.

> *Just say to covetousness that you will strangle it and rid it out of your very nature.*

Do you say, "How am I going to check covetousness?"

Well, I don't think there is any difficulty about that. If you find yourself getting very covetous, very selfish, wanting to get everything you can into your possession – just begin to scatter. Just say to covetousness that you will strangle it and rid it out of your very nature.

A wealthy farmer in New York, who was known for hoarding his wealth and being a very selfish man, was converted. Soon after his conversion, a poor man came to him and asked for help. He had lost everything and had no provisions. This young convert thought he would be generous and give him a ham from his smokehouse. He started toward the smokehouse, and on the way, the tempter said, "Give him the smallest one you have."

He struggled all the way to the smokehouse as to whether he would give a large or a small one. In order to overcome his selfishness, he took down the biggest ham he had and gave it to the man.

The tempter said, "You're a fool."

But he replied, "If you don't keep silent, I'll give him every ham I have in the smokehouse."

If you find that you are selfish, give something away. Determine to overcome that spirit of selfishness and to keep your body under, no matter what it may cost.

Henry Durant told me he was hired by Goodyear to defend the rubber patent. He would receive half of the money that came from the patent if he succeeded. One day, he woke up to find that he was a rich man. He said that the greatest struggle of his life then took place as to whether he would let money be his master or if he would be the master of his money. He had to decide whether he would be its slave or make it a slave to him. At last he got the victory, and that is how Wellesley College was built.

Are You Jealous or Envious?

Go and do something kind for the person of whom you are jealous. That's the way to cure jealousy. It will kill it. Jealousy is a devil and a horrid monster. The poets imagined that Envy dwelt in a dark cave, being pale and thin, hiding in the corner, never rejoicing except in the misfortune of others, and hurting himself continually.

There's a fable of an eagle which could outfly another, and the other didn't like it. The latter saw a sportsman one day and said to him, "I wish you would bring down that eagle."

The sportsman replied that he would if he only had

some feathers to put into his arrow. So the eagle pulled one out of his wing. The arrow was shot but didn't quite reach the rival eagle. It was flying too high. The envious eagle pulled out more feathers and kept pulling them out until he lost so many that he couldn't fly. Then the sportsman turned around and killed him. If you are jealous, the only one you can hurt is yourself.

There were two businessmen with a longstanding rivalry between them that included many bitter feelings. Then one of them was converted.

He went to his minister and said, "I'm still jealous of that man and don't know how to overcome it."

The minister replied, "Well, if a man comes into your store to buy goods, and you cannot supply him, just send him over to your neighbor."

He said, "I wouldn't like to do that."

"Well," the minister said, "you do it and you will kill jealousy."

He said he would.

When a customer came into his store for goods which he did not have, he told him to go across the street to his neighbor's store. After some time, the other man began to send his customers over to this man's store, and the breach was healed.

Pride

Then there is *pride*. This is another of those sins which the Bible so strongly condemns, but which the world hardly recognizes as a sin at all.

Haughty eyes and a proud heart, the lamp of

the wicked, is sin (Proverbs 21:4). *Everyone who is proud in heart is an abomination to the LORD; Assuredly, he will not be unpunished* (Proverbs 16:5).

Christ included pride among those evil things which proceed out of the heart of a man and defile him.

People have the idea that it's just the wealthy who are proud. Go down some of the back streets, and you will find that some of the very poorest are as proud as the richest. It is the heart, you know. People that don't have any money are just as proud as those that do. We have got to crush it out. It is an enemy. There's no need to be proud of your face, for there isn't one that will survive ten days in the grave. There's nothing to be proud of, is there? Let's ask God to deliver us from pride.

> *People that don't have any money are just as proud as those that do.*

You can't simply fold your arms and say, "Lord, take it out of me." You must work with Him.

Conquer your pride by cultivating humility. Paul exhorts us to be *as those who have been chosen of God, holy and beloved, put on a heart of compassion, kindness, humility* (Colossians 3:12). Peter reminds us to *clothe yourselves with humility toward one another, for God is opposed to the proud, but gives grace to the humble* (1 Peter 5:5). And in the Sermon on the Mount, Jesus teaches, *Blessed are the poor in spirit* (Matthew 5:3).

PART III

External Foes

What are our external foes? What does James say? *You adulteresses, do you not know that friendship with the world is hostility toward God? Therefore whoever wishes to be a friend of the world makes himself an enemy of God* (James 4:4). And John? *Do not love the world nor the things in the world. If anyone loves the world, the love of the Father is not in him* (1 John 2:15).

People want to know, when you say *the world*, what do you mean?

We find the answer in the next verse. *For all that is in the world, the lust of the flesh and the lust of the eyes and the boastful pride of life, is not from the Father, but is from the world. The world is passing away, and also its lusts; but the one who does the will of God lives forever* (1 John 2:16-17).

The world does not mean nature around us. God nowhere tells us that the material world is an enemy to be overcome. On the contrary, we read, *The earth is the LORD'S, and all it contains, the world, and those who dwell in it* (Psalm 24:1). And, *The heavens are telling of the glory of God; And their expanse is declaring the work of His hands* (Psalm 19:1).

Canon Liddon taught that "Human life and society are alienated from God, through being centered on material pursuits and possessions, and because of this are opposed to God's Spirit and kingdom." Christ said, *If the world hates you, you know that it has hated Me before it hated you. If you were of the world, the world would love its own; but because you are not of the world, but I chose you out of the world, because of this the world hates you* (John 15:18-19). Love of the world means a lack of consideration for the eternal future because of a love for passing things.

How can the world be overcome? Not by education and not by experience. It can only be overcome by faith. *For whatever is born of God overcomes the world; and this is the victory that has overcome the world -our faith. Who is the one who overcomes the world, but he who believes that Jesus is the Son of God?* (1 John 5:4-5).

Worldly Habits and Fashions

One thing we must fight is *worldly habits and fashions*. We must often go against the customs of the world. I have great respect for a man who can stand up for what he believes is right against all the world. He who can stand alone is a hero.

Suppose it is the custom for young men to do certain

things you wouldn't like your mother to know of or things your mother taught you are wrong. You may have to stand up alone among all your companions.

They will say, "You can't get away from your mother, eh? Tied to your mother's apron strings?"

Just say, "Yes, I have respect for my mother. She taught me what is right, and she's the best friend I have. I believe what you're doing is wrong, and I'm going to stand for the right." If you have to stand alone, *stand*. Enoch did it, and Joseph, and Elisha, and Paul. God has kept such men in all ages.

Someone says, "I drink socially. I know it's a dangerous thing because my son is likely to follow me. But I can stop whenever I want to. Perhaps my son hasn't got the same power as I have, and it may be too much for him. But it's the custom in the society in which I move."

Once I got into a place where I had to get up and leave. I was invited into a home, and they served a late supper. There were seven kinds of liquor on the table. I'm ashamed to say they were Christian people. A deacon urged a young lady to drink until she was embarrassed. I rose from the table and left. I felt that it was no place for me. They considered me very rude. It went against custom to protest such an infernal thing. Let's go against custom when it leads us astray.

I was told in a southern college, some years ago, that no man was considered a first-class gentleman who didn't drink. Of course it is not so now.

Pleasure

Another enemy is *worldly pleasure*. Many people are just drowned in pleasure. They have no time for any meditation at all. Many men are useless to society and to their families, because they gave themselves up to the god of pleasure. God wants His children to be happy, but in a way that will help and not hinder them.

A lady came to me once and said, "Mr. Moody, I wish you would tell me how I can become a Christian." The tears rolled down her cheeks. "But I don't want to be one of your kind."

"Well," I asked, "have I got a peculiar kind? What's the matter with my Christianity?"

"Well," she said, "my father was a doctor and had a large practice. He used to get so tired that he took us to the theater. We were a large family, and we had tickets for the theater three or four times a week. I suppose we were there a good deal more often than we were in church. Now I'm married to a lawyer, and he has a large practice. He gets so tired that he takes us out to the theater." She added, "I'm far better acquainted with the theater and theater people than with the church and church people. And I don't want to give up the theater."

"Well," I said, "did you ever hear me say anything about theaters? There have been reporters here every day for all the different papers. They print my sermons verbatim in one of the papers. Have you ever seen anything in my sermons against theaters?"

She said, "No."

"Well," I said, "I have seen you in the audience every

afternoon for several weeks, and have you heard me say anything against theaters?"

No, she hadn't.

"Well," I said, "what made you bring them up?"

"Why, I supposed you didn't believe in theaters."

"What made you think that?"

She said, "Do you ever go?"

"No."

"Why don't you go?"

"Because I've got something better. I would rather go out into the street and eat dirt than do some of the things I used to do before I became a Christian."

She said, "I don't understand."

I said, "When Jesus Christ has the position of authority, you will understand it all. He didn't come down here and say we shouldn't go here and shouldn't go there. He didn't lay down a lot of rules, but He laid down great principles. He says if you love Him you will take delight in pleasing Him." As I preached Christ to her, the tears started again.

> I would rather go out into the street and eat dirt than do some of the things I used to do before I became a Christian.

She said, "I tell you, Mr. Moody, that sermon on the indwelling Christ yesterday afternoon just broke my heart. I admire Him and want to be a Christian, but I don't want to give up the theaters."

I said, "Please don't mention them again. I don't want to talk about theaters. I want to talk to you about Christ." So I took my Bible, and I read to her about Christ.

But she said again, "Mr. Moody, can I go to the theater if I become a Christian?"

"Yes," I said, "you can go to the theater just as much as you like if you are a true Christian, and you can go with His blessing."

"Well," she said, "I am glad you are not as narrow-minded as some."

She felt quite relieved to think that she could go to the theater and be a Christian.

But I said, "If you can go to the theater for the glory of God, keep on going. But be sure that you go for the glory of God. If you are a Christian, you will be glad to do whatever pleases Him."

I really think she became a Christian that day. The burden was gone and there was joy. However, just as she left, she said, "I'm not going to give up the theater."

In a few days she came back to me and said, "Mr. Moody, I understand all about that theater business now. I went the other night. There was a large party at our house, and my husband wanted us to go. We went. But when the curtain lifted, everything looked so different. I said to my husband, 'This is no place for me. This is horrible. I'm not going to stay. I'm going home.'

"He said, 'Don't make a fool of yourself. Everyone has heard that you've been converted in the Moody meetings. If you go out, everyone will hear about that too. I beg of you, don't make a fool of yourself by getting up and going out.'

"But I said, 'I have been making a fool of myself all of my life.'"

The theater hadn't changed, but she had something better. She was going to overcome the world. *For those who are according to the flesh set their minds on the things of the flesh, but those who are according to the Spirit, the things of the Spirit* (Romans 8:5). When Christ has the first place in your heart, you are going to get victory. Just do whatever you know will please Him. The great objection I have to these things is that they are given too much importance, and become a hindrance to spiritual growth.

Business

It may be that we have to overcome in *business*. Perhaps it's business morning, noon, and night, and Sundays too. When a man drives like Jehu[1] all week and like a snail on Sunday, isn't there something wrong with him? Now, business is legitimate, and a man isn't a good citizen if he won't go out and earn his bread by the sweat of his brow. He ought to be a good businessman and do the best job possible. At the same time, if he lays his whole heart on his business, makes a god of it, and thinks more of it than anything else, then the world has come in. It may be very legitimate in its place, like fire, which, in its place, is one of the best friends of man. Out of place, however, it is one of the worst enemies of man. Like water, which we cannot live without. Yet, when not in place, it becomes an enemy.

So my friends, that's the question for you and me to settle. Now examine yourself. Are you getting the victory? Are you growing more in your Christian character? Are you achieving mastery over the world and the flesh?

---

1   *And the watchman told, saying, He came even unto them, and cometh not again: and the driving is like the driving of Jehu the son of Nimshi; for he driveth furiously* (2 Kings 9:20).

Remember that every temptation you overcome makes you stronger to overcome others. And every temptation that defeats you makes you weaker. You can become weaker and weaker or stronger and stronger. Sin takes the strength out of your vitality, but godly character makes you stronger. So many men have been overcome by some little thing. Remember what it tells us in the Song of Solomon. *Catch the foxes for us, the little foxes that are ruining the vineyards, while our vineyards are in blossom* (Song of Solomon 2:15). Many people seem to think that things like getting agitated, being misleading, and telling white lies are little things. Sometimes you are able to stand strong in the face of a great temptation, and before you know it, you fall when faced with some little thing. Many men are overcome by a little *persecution*.

> *Remember that every temptation you overcome makes you stronger to overcome others.*

Persecution

I don't think we have enough persecution today. Some people say we have persecution that is just as hard to bear as in the Dark Ages. Anyway, I think it would be a good thing if we had a little of the old-fashioned kind about now. It would bring out the strongest characters and make us all healthier. I have heard men get up in a prayer meeting, say they were going to make a few remarks, and then keep on till you would think they were going to talk all week. If we had a little persecution, people like that wouldn't talk so much. Spurgeon used to say some Christians would make good martyrs.

They would burn well, because they are so dry. If there were a few stakes for burning Christians, I think it would take all the religiousness out of some men. I admit they haven't got much to start with. If they aren't willing to suffer a little persecution for Christ, they aren't fit to be His disciples. We are told, *Indeed, all who desire to live godly in Christ Jesus will be persecuted* (2 Timothy 3:12). If the world has nothing to say against you, Jesus Christ will have nothing to say for you.

The most glorious triumphs of the church have been won in times of persecution. The early church was persecuted for about three hundred years after the crucifixion. Those were years of growth and progress. But then, as Saint Augustine has said, the cross passed from the scene of public executions to the crown of the Caesars, and the downgrade movement began. When the church joined hands with the State, it consistently deteriorated in spirituality and effectiveness. However, the opposition of the State only served to purify it of all impurity. It was persecution that gave Scotland to Presbyterianism. It was persecution that gave this country to civil and religious freedom.

How are we to overcome in time of persecution? Hear the words of Christ. *These things I have spoken to you, so that in Me you may have peace. In the world you have tribulation, but take courage; I have overcome the world* (John 16:33). Paul could testify that, though persecuted, he was never forsaken. The Lord stood by him, strengthened him, and delivered him out of all his persecutions and afflictions.

Many shrink from the Christian life because they will be mocked. Then sometimes when persecution won't bring a man down, flattery will. Foolish people often come up to a man after he has preached and flatter him. Sometimes ladies do that. Perhaps they will say to some worker in the church, "You talk a great deal better than so-and-so." He becomes proud and struts around as if he was the most important person in the town. I tell you, we have a wily Devil to contend with. If he can't overcome you with opposition, he will try flattery or ambition. If that doesn't serve his purpose, perhaps there will come some affliction or disappointment, and he will overcome in that way. Remember, anyone that has Christ to help him can overcome every foe and overcome them singly or collectively. Let them come. If we have Christ within us, we will overthrow them all. Remember what Christ is able to do. In all the ages, men have stood in greater temptations than you and I will ever have to meet.

Anyone that has Christ to help him can overcome every foe.

There is one more thing to consider. I have to overcome the world, or the world is going to overcome me. I have to conquer sin in me and get it under my feet, or it is going to conquer me. Some people are satisfied with one or two victories and think that's good enough. We have got to do something more than that. It's a battle all the time. We can be encouraged by the fact that we are assured of victory in the end. We are promised a glorious triumph.

To Him That Overcomes

In the book of Revelation, the author makes eight promises to those who overcome in this life.

To him who overcomes, I will grant to eat of the tree of life which is in the Paradise of God (Revelation 2:7). He will have a right to the tree of life. When Adam fell, he lost that right. God turned him out of Eden so that he couldn't eat of the tree of life and live forever. Perhaps He took that tree and transplanted it to the garden above. Through the second Adam, we are offered the right to eat of it.

He who overcomes will not be hurt by the second death (Revelation 2:11). Death holds no power over him. It cannot touch him. Why? Because Christ tasted death, and through His death gained victory for every man. Death may take this body, but that is all. This is only the house I live in. We should have no fear of death if we overcome.

To him who overcomes, to him I will give some of the hidden manna, and I will give him a white stone, and a new name written on the stone which no one knows but he who receives it (Revelation 2:17). If I overcome, God will feed me with bread that the world knows nothing about, and He will give me a new name.

He who overcomes, and he who keeps My deeds until the end, to him I will give authority over the nations (Revelation 2:26). Think of it. What a thing to have, power over the nations. A man that is able to rule himself is the man that God can trust with power. Only a man who can govern himself is fit to govern other men. It seems like we are down here in training, and God is just polishing us for higher service. The details may not be specific, but God's Word tells us that we will reign with Him.

He who overcomes will thus be clothed in white garments; and I will not erase his name from the book of life, and I will confess his name before My Father and before His angels (Revelation 3:5). Jesus will present us to the Father in white garments, without spot or wrinkle. Every fault and stain will be removed. We will be made perfect. He that overcomes will not be a stranger in heaven.

He who overcomes, I will make him a pillar in the temple of My God, and he will not go out from it anymore; and I will write on him the name of My God, and the name of the city of My God, the new Jerusalem, which comes down out of heaven from My God, and My new name (Revelation 3:12). Imagine no more backsliding and no more wandering over the dark mountains of sin. We will be forever with the King.

He says, *I will write on him the name of my God.*

He is going to put His name on us. Isn't it grand? That is something worth fighting for.

It is said that when Muhammad came in sight of Damascus and found that the people had all left the city, he said, "If they won't fight for this city, what will they fight for?" If men won't fight here for all this reward, what will they fight for?

He who overcomes, I will grant to him to sit down with Me on My throne, as I also overcame and sat down with My Father on His throne (Revelation 3:21). My heart has often melted as I have looked at that passage. The Lord of glory comes down and says, "I will grant to you to sit on My throne, even as I sit on My Father's throne, if you will just overcome." Isn't it worth a struggle? Countless many fight for a crown that will fade away. Yet, we are to be placed above the angels, archangels, seraphim, and cherubim. We will be placed upon the throne, and we will remain forever with Him. May God put strength into every one of us to fight the battle of life, so we may *Isn't it worth a struggle?* sit with Him on His throne. When Emperor Frederick III of Germany was dying, his own son would not have been allowed to sit with him on the throne. Nor did the son have the authority to let anyone else sit there with him. Yet, we are told that we are joint heirs with Jesus Christ, and we will sit with Him in glory.

Finally, *He who overcomes will inherit these things, and I will be his God and he will be My son* (Revelation 21:7). My dear friends, isn't that a high calling? I used to have my Sunday school children sing, "I want to be an angel," but have not done so for years. We will be above angels. We will be sons of God. We will inherit all things. Do you ask how much I'm worth? I don't know. The Rothschilds cannot compute their wealth. They don't even know how many millions they own. My condition is the same. I haven't the slightest idea how much I'm worth. God has no poor children. If we overcome, we will inherit all things.

What an inheritance. Let's get the victory through Jesus Christ, our Lord and Master.

Part IV

Repentance

Results of True Repentance

I want to draw your attention to what true repentance leads to. I'm not addressing the unconverted only, because I believe that there is a good deal of repentance to be done by the church before much will be accomplished in the world. I firmly believe that the low standard of Christian living is keeping many enslaved to the world and bound in their sins. When the ungodly see Christian people who do not repent, it's unreasonable to expect them to repent and turn away from their sins. I have repented thousands of times more since I've known Christ than ever before. I think most Christians have some things to repent of.

This lesson applies to Christians, to myself, and to anyone who has never accepted Christ as his Savior.

There are five things that flow out of true repentance:

1. Conviction.

2. Contrition.

3. Confession of sin.

4. Conversion.

5. Confession of Jesus Christ before the world.

Conviction

When a man is not deeply convicted of sin, it is a pretty sure sign that he has not truly repented. Experience has taught me that men who have very little conviction of sin, sooner or later lapse back into their old life. For the last few years, I have experienced a growing burden for a deep and true growth in professing converts far more than for impressive numbers. If a man professes to be converted without realizing the enormity of his sins, he is likely to be one of those stony-ground hearers who don't amount to anything (Matthew 13:5-6). The first indication of opposition, or the first wave of persecution or ridicule, will suck them back into the world again.

I believe we are making a woeful mistake by taking so many people into the church who have never truly been convicted of sin. Sin is just as black in many mens' hearts today as it ever was. I sometimes think it's blacker. The more understanding a man has, the greater his responsibility, and therefore the greater his need for deep conviction.

William Dawson once told this story to illustrate how humble the soul must be before it can find peace.

At a revival meeting, a little lad who was used to Methodist ways, went home to his mother and said, "Mother, John So-and-so is under conviction and seeking peace, but he won't find it tonight, Mother."

"Why, William?" she asked.

"Because he is only down on one knee, Mother, and he will never get peace until he is down on both knees."

Until conviction of sin brings us down on both knees, until we are completely humbled, until we have no hope in ourselves left, we cannot find the Savior.

Conscience, the Word of God, and the Holy Spirit lead a person to conviction. All three are used by God.

Long before we had the Scriptures, God dealt with men through the conscience. That's what made Adam and Eve hide themselves from the presence of the Lord God among the trees of the garden of

Until conviction of sin brings us down on both knees, we cannot find the Savior.

Eden. It's what convicted Joseph's brothers when they acknowledged their guilt twenty years after they sold him into slavery. *Then they said to one another, Truly we are guilty concerning our brother, because we saw the distress of his soul when he pleaded with us, yet we would not listen; therefore this distress has come upon us* (Genesis 42:21). We must appeal to the conscience of our children before they are old enough to understand about the Scriptures and the Spirit of God. The conscience is what accuses or excuses the heathen.

Conscience is a divinely implanted ability in man, telling him that he ought to do right. Someone once said it was born when Adam and Eve ate the forbidden fruit, when their eyes were opened and they knew *good and evil* (Genesis 3:22). It passes judgment without being invited. It approves or condemns our thoughts, words, and actions, and judges them to be right or wrong. A man cannot violate his conscience without being self-condemned.

However, conscience is not a safe guide, because often it won't tell you a thing is wrong until you've already done it. It needs God's influence because it's a partner with our fallen nature. Many people do things that are wrong without being condemned by conscience. *I thought to myself that I had to do many things hostile to the name of Jesus of Nazareth* (Acts 26:9). Conscience itself needs to be educated.

Again, conscience is too often like an alarm clock. It awakens and arouses at first, but after time the man becomes used to it, and it loses its effect. Conscience can be smothered. I think we make a mistake by not preaching more to the conscience, aiming to convict with our words.

Over the course of time, conscience was replaced by the law of God, which was fulfilled in Christ.

Now, the masses have access to Bibles, and these are the instrument by which God produces conviction. The Word of God tells you what is right and wrong *before* you commit sin. It is critical that we learn and embrace its teachings, under the guidance of the Holy Spirit. Conscience compared with the Bible is like a flashlight compared with the sun in the heavens.

The truth convicted those Jews on the day of Pentecost. Peter, filled with the Holy Spirit, preached *that God has made Him both Lord and Christ -this Jesus whom you crucified. Now when they heard this, they were pierced to the heart, and said to Peter and the rest of the apostles, Brethren, what shall we do?* (Acts 2:36-37).

Finally, the Holy Spirit convicts. *And He* [the Comforter] *when He comes, will convict the world concerning sin and righteousness and judgment; concerning sin, because they do not believe in Me* (John 16:8-9).

I once heard the late Dr. A. J. Gordon teach on this passage. He said, "Some commentators say there was no real conviction of sin in the world until the Holy Spirit came. I think that foreign missionaries will disagree. A heathen who never heard of Christ may have a tremendous conviction of sin. Notice that God gave conscience first and gave the Comforter afterward. Conscience bears witness to the law. The Comforter bears witness to Christ. Conscience brings legal conviction. The Comforter brings scriptural conviction. Conscience brings conviction to the point of condemnation. And the Comforter brings conviction unto salvation. He shall convince the world of sin because they don't believe in Me. That's the sin about which He convinces. It does not say that He convinces men of sin because they have stolen or lied or committed adultery. The Holy Spirit is to convince men of sin, because they have not believed in Jesus Christ. The coming of Jesus Christ into the world made a sin possible that was not possible before. Light reveals darkness. It takes whiteness to bring conviction concerning blackness. There are natives in Central Africa who never dreamed that they were dark-skinned until they saw the face of a white man. A great many people in this world never knew they were sinful until they saw the face of Jesus Christ in all its purity.

"Jesus Christ now stands between us and the law. He has fulfilled the law for us and settled all claims it had on us. Whatever claim it had on us has been transferred to Him. It is no longer the *sin* question, but the *Son* question, that confronts us. The first thing Peter does when he begins to preach after the Holy Spirit has been sent down is proclaim Christ. *This Man, delivered over by the predetermined plan and foreknowledge of God, you nailed to a cross by the hands of godless men and put Him to death* (Acts 2:23). It doesn't say a word about any other kind of sin. That's the sin that runs all through Peter's teaching. As he preached, the Holy Spirit came down and convicted them, and they cried out, *What shall we do to be saved?*

"We had no part in crucifying Christ. So what is *our* sin? It is the same sin in another form. They were convicted of crucifying Christ. We are convicted because we have not believed in Christ crucified. They were convicted because they despised and rejected God's Son. The Holy Spirit convicts us because we have not believed in the Despised and Rejected One. It's really the same sin in both cases – the sin of unbelief in Christ."

Some of the most powerful meetings I've ever been in were those in which there came a sort of hush over the people, and it seemed like an unseen power gripped their consciences. I remember a man who came to one meeting. The moment he entered, he felt that God was there. A sense of awe came upon him, and that very hour he was convicted and converted.

Contrition

Contrition is a deep, godly sorrow and humiliation of heart because of sin. If there isn't true contrition, a man will turn right back to his old sin. That's the trouble with many Christians.

A man may get angry, and if there isn't contrition, the next day he will get angry again. A daughter may say mean, cutting things to her mother. Then her conscience troubles her, and she says, "Mother, I am sorry. Please forgive me."

If there isn't true contrition, a man will turn right back to his old sin.

But soon there's another outburst of temper, because the contrition is not deep and real. A husband speaks sharp words to his wife. Then to ease his conscience, he goes and buys her a bouquet of flowers. He will not go like a man and admit his behavior was wrong.

What God wants is contrition. If there isn't contrition, there isn't full repentance. *The LORD is near to the brokenhearted and saves those who are crushed in spirit* (Psalm 34:18). *A broken and a contrite heart, O God, You will not despise* (Psalm 51:17). Many sinners are sorry for their sins, sorry they cannot continue in them. They repent only with hearts that are not broken. I don't think we know *how* to repent today.

We need a modern-day John the Baptist wandering through the land crying, "Repent! Repent!"

Confession of Sin

True contrition will lead us to confess our sins. I believe nine-tenths of the trouble in our Christian life comes from failing to do this. We try to hide and cover up our sins, but there is very little confession of them. Someone said, "Unconfessed sin in the soul is like a bullet in the body."

If you are not experiencing the power of God in your life, you may have unconfessed sin or something in your life that needs straightening out. There is no amount of psalm-singing, attending religious meetings, praying, or reading your Bible that is going to cover up anything of that kind. It must be confessed. If I am too proud to confess, I shouldn't expect mercy from God or answers to my prayers. *He who conceals his transgressions will not prosper, but he who confesses and forsakes them will find compassion* (Proverbs 28:13). He may be a man in the pulpit, a priest behind the altar, or a king on the throne, but covered-up sin has consequences. Man has been trying to cover up sin for six thousand years. Adam tried it, and failed. Moses tried it when he buried the Egyptian he killed, but he failed. *Be sure your sin will find you out* (Numbers 32:23b). You can bury your sin as deep as you like, but it will keep coming to the surface if it has not been blotted out by the Son of God. What man has failed to do for six thousand years, you and I had better give up trying to do.

There are three ways of confessing sin. All sin is against God and must be confessed to Him. Some sins I never have to confess to anyone on earth. If the sin has been between myself and God, I may confess it alone in my closet. I don't even have to whisper it in the ear of any mortal. *And the son said to him, Father, I have sinned against heaven and in your sight; I am no longer worthy to be called your son* (Luke 15:21). *Against You, You only, I have sinned and done what is evil in Your sight* (Psalm 51:4).

However, if I have done some man a wrong, and he knows that I have wronged him, I must confess that sin not only to God but also to that man. If I have too much pride to confess it to him, I don't even need to go to God. I may pray and weep, but it won't do any good. First, confess to that man. Then go to God and see how quickly He will hear you and send peace. *Therefore if you are presenting your offering at the altar, and there remember that your brother has something against you, leave your offering there before the altar and go; first be reconciled to your brother, and then come and present your offering* (Matthew 5:23-24). That is the Scripture way.

There is another class of sins that must be confessed publicly. If I have been known as a blasphemer, a drunkard, or a shameless sinner, and I repent of my sins, I owe the public a confession. The confession should be as public as the transgression. Many people will say something mean about another in the presence of others, and then try to patch it up by going to that person privately. The confession should be made so that all who heard the transgression can hear it.

We are far too concerned about confessing other people's sins. If we are interested in true repentance, we will have as much as we can handle to look after our own. When a man or woman gets a good look into God's looking glass, he doesn't find fault with other people as much as he does in himself.

If we confess our sins, He is faithful and righteous to forgive us our sins and to cleanse us from all unrighteousness (1 John 1:9). Thank God for the gospel. If there is any sin in your life, make up your mind to confess it and be forgiven. Don't have any cloud between you and God. Know you have a clear title to the mansion Christ has gone to prepare for you.

Don't have any cloud between you and God.

Conversion

Confession leads to true conversion. There is no conversion at all until these three steps have been taken.

The word *conversion* means two things. We say a man is converted when he is born again. But it also has a different meaning in the Bible.

Peter said, *Therefore repent and return* (Acts 3:19). The Revised Version reads, *Repent therefore, and turn.* Paul said that he was not disobedient unto the heavenly vision, but preached to Jews and Gentiles that they should repent and *turn* to God.

An old theologian once said, "Every man is born with his back to God. Repentance is a change of one's course. It is right about face."

Sin is a turning away from God. It is *aversion* from God and *conversion* to the world. True repentance means conversion to God and aversion from the world. When there is true contrition, the heart is broken *for* sin. When there is true conversion, the heart is broken *from* sin. We leave the old life and are transferred out of the kingdom of darkness into the kingdom of light. Wonderful, isn't it?

Unless our repentance includes this conversion, it's not worth much. If a man continues in sin, it's proof of an idle profession. It's like pumping away at the ship's pumps without stopping the leaks. Solomon said, *And they pray toward this place and confess Your name and turn from their sin when You afflict them* (1 Kings 8:35). Prayer and confession would be ineffective while they continued in sin. Let us listen to God's call and forsake the old, wicked way. Let us return to the Lord. He will have mercy on us and pardon us.

If you have never turned to God, turn now. I disagree with the idea that it takes six months, or six weeks, or six hours to be converted. It doesn't take you very long to turn around, does it? If you know you are wrong, then turn around.

Confession of Christ

If you are converted, the next step is to confess it openly. *If you confess with your mouth Jesus as Lord, and believe in your heart that God raised Him from the dead, you will be saved; for with the heart a person believes, resulting in righteousness, and with the mouth he confesses, resulting in salvation* (Romans 10:9-10).

Confession of Christ is the completion of the work of true repentance. We owe it to the world, to our fellow Christians, and to ourselves. He *died* to redeem us. Should we be ashamed or afraid to confess Him? Religion as a concept – as a doctrine – holds little interest for the world, but what people can say from personal experience always has weight.

I remember taking part in meetings where the truth was met with resistance. Bitter and reproachful things were being exchanged.

But one day, one of the most prominent men in the room rose and said, "I want it to be known that I am a disciple of Jesus Christ. If there is any condemnation to be cast on His cause, I'm prepared to take my share of it."

It went through the meeting like an electric current, and a blessing came at once to his soul and to the souls of others.

You've got to make a public confession when you accept Christ. You must confess Him in your place of business and in your family. Let the whole world know that you are on His side.

Many are willing to accept Christ, but they are not willing to confess it. Many are too focused on the lions and the bears in the way. Now, my friends, the Devil's mountains are only made of smoke. He can throw a straw into your path and make a mountain of it.

He says, "You can't confess to your *family*. You'll break down. You can't tell your coworker. He'll laugh at you."

But when you accept Christ, you will have the power to confess Him.

There was a young man in the West who pondered his soul's salvation. One afternoon in his office, he said, "I will accept Jesus Christ as my Lord and Savior."

He went home and told his wife (who was a nominal

professor of religion) that he made up his mind to serve Christ, and added, "After supper tonight I'm going to take our company into the living room and erect a family altar."

"Well," said his wife, "you know some of the gentlemen who are coming to tea are sceptics, and they are older than you. Don't you think you'd better wait until after they leave, or go into the kitchen and have your first prayer with the servants?"

The young man thought for a few moments and said, "I've asked Jesus Christ into my house for the first time, and I will take Him into the best room, not into the kitchen."

So he called his friends into the drawing room. There was a little mocking, but he read and prayed. That man became chief justice of the United States Supreme Court. *For I am not ashamed of the gospel, for it is the power of God for salvation to everyone who believes* (Romans 1:16).

A young man enlisted and was sent to his regiment. The first night he was in the barracks with about fifteen other young men who passed the time playing cards and gambling. Before retiring, he fell on his knees and prayed. They cursed at him, taunted him, and threw their boots at him.

So it went on the next night and the next. Finally, the young man went and told the chaplain what took place and asked what he should do.

"Well," said the chaplain, "you aren't at home now, and the other men have just as much right in the barracks as you have. It makes them mad to hear you pray. The Lord will hear you just as well if you say your prayers in bed and don't provoke them."

For weeks, the chaplain didn't see the young man.

Finally, he saw him and asked, "By the way, did you take my advice?"

"I did, for two or three nights."

"How did it work?"

"Well," said the young man, "I felt like a whipped hound. So the third night I got out of bed, knelt down, and prayed."

"Well," asked the chaplain, "how did that work?"

The young soldier answered, "We now have a prayer meeting every night. Three have been converted, and we are praying for the rest."

I am so tired of weak Christianity.
I am so tired of weak Christianity. Let's be all-out for Christ. If the world wants to call us fools, let them do it. It's only for a little while. The crowning day is coming. Thank God for the privilege we have of confessing Christ.

True Wisdom

Those who have insight will shine brightly like the brightness of the expanse of heaven, and those who lead the many to righteousness, like the stars forever and ever (Daniel 12:3).

That is the testimony of an old man. He had the richest and deepest experience of any man living on the face of the earth at the time. He was taken to Babylon when he was a young man. Some Bible students think he wasn't more than twenty years old. If anyone had said, when this young Hebrew was carried away into captivity, that he would outrank all the mighty men of that day, no one would have believed it. All the generals who had been victorious in almost every nation at that time would be eclipsed by this young slave. Yet for five hundred years, no man whose life is recorded in history shone like his. He exceeded Nebuchadnezzar, Belshazzar, Cyrus, Darius, and all the princes and mighty monarchs of his day.

We aren't told when he was converted to a knowledge of the true God, but I think we have good reason to believe that it happened under the influence of Jeremiah the prophet. Evidently, some earnest, godly man made a deep impression on him. *Someone* taught him how he was to serve God.

We hear people nowadays talk about the hardness of the field where they labor. They say their position is a very peculiar one. Think of the field in which Daniel had to work. He wasn't only a slave, but he also was held captive by a nation that detested the Hebrews. The language was unknown to him. And there he was among idolaters. Yet he took his stand for God from the very beginning and went on through his whole life that way. He gave the dew of his youth to God and continued faithfully right on until his pilgrimage ended.

Notice that all those who have made a deep impression on the world, and have shone most brightly, have been men who lived in a dark day. Look at Joseph. He was sold as a slave into Egypt by the Ishmaelites. Yet he took his God with him into captivity just as Daniel later did. And he remained true to the end. He didn't give up his faith because he was taken away from home and placed among idolaters. He stood firm, and God stood by him.

Look at Moses, who turned his back upon the gilded

palaces of Egypt. He identified himself with his despised and downtrodden nation. If ever a man had a hard field, it was Moses. Yet he shone brightly and proved faithful to God.

Elijah lived in a far darker day than we do. The whole nation was turning to idolatry. Ahab, his queen, and all the royal court threw their influence *against* the worship of the true God. Yet Elijah stood firm and shone brightly in that dark and evil day. Now his name stands out on the pages of history.

Consider John the Baptist. I used to think I would like to live in the days of the prophets, but I have given up that idea. You can be sure that when a prophet appears on the scene, everything is dark, and the professing church of God has gone over to the service of the god of this world. So it was, when John the Baptist made his appearance. See how his name shines out today. More than eighteen centuries have rolled away, and the fame of that wilderness preacher shines brighter than ever. He was looked down upon in his day and generation, but he has outlived all his enemies. His name will be revered and his work remembered for as long as the church is on the earth.

Talk about a hard field. Paul shone for God as he went out as the first missionary to the heathen. He told them of the God he served, and who had sent His Son to die a cruel death in order to save the world. Men reviled him and his teachings. They laughed at him and mocked him when he spoke of the crucified One. But he kept preaching the gospel of the Son of God. He was regarded as a poor tentmaker by the great and mighty ones of his day.

However, no one can recall the name of any of his persecutors unless their names happen to be associated with his.

The fact is, *all* men like to shine. We may as well acknowledge that now. Men struggle to get to the top of the ladder in business. Everyone wants to outshine his neighbor and to stand at the head of his profession. In the political world, there is always a struggle going on as to who shall be the greatest. Even in schools, you will find a rivalry between the boys and girls. They all want to stand at the top of the class. When a boy reaches a position where he outranks all the rest, the mother is very proud of it. She manages to tell all the neighbors about how well Johnny has done, and what awards he has received.

In the army you find one trying to outstrip the other. Everyone is very anxious to shine and rise above his comrades. The young men are anxious to outdo the other in their games. So we all have that desire in us. We like to shine above others.

However, there are very few who can actually shine in the world. Once in a while one man will outstrip all his competitors. Every four years, a struggle goes on throughout our country to determine who will be the president of the United States. The battle rages for six months or a year. Yet only one man can get the prize. Many struggle to get the position, but most are disappointed, because only one can attain the coveted prize. But in the kingdom of God the very least and the very weakest can shine if they will. Not only can *one* obtain the prize, but *all* may have it if they will.

It doesn't say in this passage that the statesmen will shine as the brightness of God's kingdom. The statesmen of Babylon are gone. Even their names are forgotten.

It doesn't say that the nobility will shine. Earth's nobility are soon forgotten. John Bunyan, the Bedford tinker, has outlived the whole crowd of those who were the nobility in his day. They lived for self, and their memory is blotted out. He lived for God and for souls, and his name is as fragrant as it ever was.

We aren't told that the merchants will shine. Who can name any of the millionaires of Daniel's day? Their names were all buried in oblivion a few years after their death. Who were the mighty conquerors of that day? We can name a few. It's true that we know of Nebuchadnezzar, but it's Daniel, not Nebuchadnezzar, who stands as the giant in the faith, despite the fact that they were both used by God during the same time in Israel's history.[2]

What a different story it is with this faithful prophet of the Lord. Twenty-five centuries have passed away, and his name shines on, and on, and on, brighter and brighter. And it will continue to shine as long as the church of God exists. *Those who have insight will shine brightly like the brightness of the expanse of heaven, and those who lead the many to righteousness, like the stars forever and ever* (Daniel 12:3).

The glory of this world quickly fades away. Napoleon, the French military and political leader, almost made the earth tremble. He blazed and shone as an earthly warrior for a little while. After a few years passed, a little island

---

2   Original: It's true that we know of Nebuchadnezzar, but we probably only know of him because of his relation to the prophet Daniel.

held the once proud and mighty conqueror. He died a poor, brokenhearted prisoner. Where is he today? Almost forgotten. Who in all the world would say that Napoleon lives in their heart's affections?

But look at this despised and hated Hebrew prophet. They put him into the lions' den because he was too righteous and too religious. Yet the memory of him is still fresh today. His name is loved and honored for his faithfulness to God.

Many years ago, I was in Paris at the time of the Great Exhibition. Napoleon III was then in his glory. Cheer after cheer rose as he drove along the streets of the city. A few short years later, and *God left us here to shine.* he fell from his lofty estate. He died an exile from his country and his throne, and where is his name today? Very few think about him at all. If his name *is* mentioned, it is not with love and esteem. How empty and short-lived are the glory and pride of this world. If we are wise, we will live for God and eternity. We will get outside of ourselves and care nothing for the honor and glory of this world. *The fruit of the righteous is a tree of life, and he who is wise wins souls* (Proverbs 11:30). If any man, woman, or child by a godly life and example can win one soul to God, their life will not have been a failure. They will have outshone all the mighty men of their day, because they will have set a stream in motion that will flow on and on throughout eternity.

God left us here to shine. We are not here to buy and sell, accumulate wealth, or acquire worldly position. If we are Christians, this earth is not our home. *For our citizenship is in heaven, from which also we eagerly wait for a Savior, the Lord Jesus Christ* (Philippians 3:20). God sent us into the world to shine for Him and light up this dark world. Christ came to be the Light of the World, but men put out that light. They took it to Calvary, and blew it out.

Before Christ went up on high, He said to His disciples, *You are the light of the world. Go therefore and make disciples of all the nations* (Matthew 5:14; 28:19).

God has called us to shine just as much as Daniel was sent into Babylon to shine. Let no man or woman say that they can't shine, because they don't have as much influence as others may have. God wants you to use the influence you have. Daniel probably didn't have much influence in Babylon at first, but God soon gave him more, because he was faithful and used what he had.

Remember, a small light will do a lot when it's in a very dark place. Put one little candle in the middle of a large room, and it will give a good deal of light.

Out in the prairie regions, when meetings were held at night in the log schoolhouses, the meetings were held by candlelight.

The first man who came brought a strip of tallow-soaked cloth with him to burn. It was perhaps all he had, but he brought it and set it on the desk. It didn't light the building much, but it was better than nothing at all. Each household brought their candle. By the time the schoolhouse was full, there was plenty of light. So if we all shine a little, there will be a good deal of light. That's what God wants us to do. If we can't all be lighthouses, all of us can at least be a tallow candle.

Sometimes, a little light will do a great deal. The city of Chicago was set on fire by a cow that kicked over a lamp, and a hundred thousand people were burnt out of house and home. Don't let Satan take advantage of you and make you think that because you can't do great things you can't do anything at all.

We must remember that we are supposed to *let* our light shine. It doesn't say, *make* your light shine. You don't have to *make* light to shine. All you have to do is to *let* it shine.

I remember hearing of a man at sea who was very seasick. In my opinion, if there is a time when a man feels that he can't do any work for the Lord, it is then. While this man was sick, he heard that someone had fallen overboard. He wondered if he could do anything to help save the man. He laid hold of a light and held it up to the porthole. The drowning man was saved. When this man got over his seasickness, he went on deck and talked with the man who was rescued. The saved man gave this testimony. He said he had already gone down a second time, and was going down for the last time when he put out his hand. Just then, someone held a light at the porthole. The light fell on his hand, and a sailor grabbed it and pulled him into the lifeboat.

It seemed like a small thing to do, but it saved the man's life. If you can't do great things, you can hold the light for some poor, perishing drunkard, who may be won to Christ and delivered from destruction. Let's take the torch of salvation into dark homes and hold up Christ to the people as the Savior of the world. If the perishing masses will be reached, we must come alongside them and pray with them and labor for them. I wouldn't give much for a man's Christianity if he isn't willing to try and save others. It is utter ingratitude if we don't reach out our hand to others who are down in the same pit

If we all did what we could, we could make a difference.

from which we were delivered. Who is able to reach and help drinking men like those who have themselves been slaves to alcohol? Won't you go out today and attempt to rescue these men? If we all did what we could, we could make a difference.

I remember reading about a blind man who sat at the corner of a street in a great city with a lantern beside him. Seeing he was blind, someone asked why he had the lantern, since the light was the same to him as the darkness.

The blind man replied, "I have it so that no one will stumble over me."

Where one man reads the Bible, a hundred read you and me. That's what Paul meant when he said we must be living epistles of Christ, known and read of all men (2 Corinthians 3:2). I wouldn't give much for all that can be done by sermons, if we don't preach Christ by our lives. If we don't present the gospel to people by our holy walk and conversation, we will not win them to Christ. A little act of kindness will possibly have more influence on them than any number of long sermons.

A vessel was caught in a storm on Lake Erie, and they were trying to reach the harbor of Cleveland. At the entrance of that port they had what are called the upper and lower lights. In the distance on the bluffs, the upper lights burned brightly. But when they neared the harbor they couldn't see the lights showing the entrance to it. The pilot thought they should return to the lake. The captain was sure they would go down if they went back, and he urged the pilot to do what he could to enter the harbor. The pilot said there was very little hope of making it into the harbor, because he had nothing to guide him. They tried everything to get the vessel in. She rode on top of the waves, then into the trough of the sea, and at last they found themselves stranded on the beach, where the vessel was dashed to pieces. Someone had neglected the lower lights, and they had gone out.

Let us take warning. God keeps the upper lights burning as brightly as ever, but He has left us down here to keep the lower lights burning. Our job is to represent Him here, as Christ represents us before the Father. I sometimes think that if we had as poor a representative in the courts above as God has down here on earth, we would have a pretty poor chance of heaven. Let's prepare for action and burn our lights brightly, so others may see the way and not stumble around in darkness.

I heard about a man in the state of Minnesota who was caught in a fearful storm. That state is cursed with winter storms which sweep down so suddenly that it makes escape difficult. The snow falls, and the wind beats it into the face of the traveler so that he can't see two feet ahead. Many men have been lost on the prairies when they were caught in one of those storms.

This man was caught and was almost to the point of giving up, when he saw a little light in a log house. He managed to get there and found a shelter from the fury of the tempest. He is now a wealthy man. As soon as he was able, he bought the farm and built a beautiful house on the spot where the log building stood. On top of a tower he installed a revolving light. Every night a storm comes, he lights it in the hope that it may be the means of saving someone else.

That is true gratitude, and that's what God wants us to do. If He rescued us and brought us up out of the horrible pit, let us always look to see if there is someone else we can help save.

Two men had charge of a revolving light in a lighthouse on a rockbound and stormy coast. Somehow the machinery went wrong, and the light didn't revolve. They were so concerned that those at sea would mistake it for some other light that they manually rotated the light through the night to keep the light moving round.

Let us keep our lights in the proper place, so that the world may see that Christianity is not a sham but a reality. In the Grecian sports, they had one game where the men ran with lights. They lit a torch at the altar, and ran a certain distance. Sometimes they were on horseback. If a man came in with his light still burning, he received a prize. If his light had gone out, he lost the prize.

Many in their old age have lost their light and their joy. They once burned and shone brightly in their families, in Sunday school, and in the church. But the world or self has come in between them and God, and their light has gone out. If you are one who has had this experience, God can help you come back to the altar of the Savior's love and light your torch again. Then you can go to those in need, and let the light of the gospel shine in those dark homes.

If we only lead one other soul to Jesus Christ, we may set a stream in motion that will flow on when we are dead and gone. Way up on the mountainside there is a little spring. It seems so small that an ox might drink it up in one drink. Then it becomes a stream, and other streams run into it. Before long it's a large brook, and then it becomes a broad river sweeping onward to the sea. On its banks are cities, towns, and villages where many thousands live. Vegetation flourishes on every side, and commerce is carried down its stately pathway to distant lands.

So if you turn one to Christ, that one may turn a hundred, and they may turn a thousand. So the stream, small at first, goes on broadening and deepening as it rolls toward eternity.

> *And I heard a voice from heaven, saying,*
> *Write, Blessed are the dead who die in the*
> *Lord from now on! Yes, says the Spirit, so*
> *that they may rest from their labors, for their*
> *deeds follow with them* (Revelation 14:13).

Many are mentioned in Scripture of whom we read that they lived so many years and then they died. The cradle and the grave are brought close together. They lived and they died, and that is all we know about them. In *these* days, you could write on the tombstone of many professing Christians the date they were born and the date they died. There is nothing in between.

You can't bury a good man's influence. It lives on. They have not buried Daniel. His influence is as great today as it ever was. Do you tell me that Joseph is dead? His influence still lives and will continue to live on and on. You can bury the frail house of clay that a good man lives in, but you can't get rid of his influence and example. Paul was never more powerful than he is today.

Do you tell me that John Howard, who went into so many of the dark prisons in Europe, is dead? Is Henry Martyn or William Wilberforce or John Bunyan dead? Go into the southern states, and there you will find millions of men and women who once were slaves. Mention to any of them the name of Wilberforce, and see how quickly their faces light up. He lived for something besides himself, and his memory will live on in the hearts of those for whom he lived and labored.

Are Wesley or Whitefield dead? The names of those great evangelists were never more honored than they are now. Is John Knox dead? You can go to any part of Scotland today and feel the power of his influence.

The enemies of these servants of God are dead. Those who persecuted them and told lies about them are dead. But the men themselves have outlived all the lies that were uttered concerning them. Not only that, but they will also shine in another world. *Those who have insight will shine brightly like the brightness of the expanse of heaven, and those who lead the many to righteousness, like the stars forever and ever* (Daniel 12:3).

Let's continue to turn as many as we can to righteousness. Let's be dead to the world, to its lies, its pleasures, and its ambitions. Let's live for God, continually going forth to win souls for Him.

Dr. Chalmers said, "Thousands of men breathe, move, and live, pass off the stage of life, and are heard of no more. Why? they do not partake of good in the world, and none were blessed by them; none could point to them as the means of their redemption: not a line they wrote, not a word they spoke, could be recalled; and so they perished: their light went out in darkness, and they were not remembered more than insects of yesterday. Will you thus live and die, O man immortal? Live for something. Do good, and leave behind you a monument of virtue that the storm of time can never destroy. Write your name, in kindness, love, and mercy, on the hearts of thousands you come in contact with year by year: you will never be forgotten. No! your name, your deeds, will be as legible on the hearts you leave behind you as the stars on the brow of evening. Good deeds will shine as the stars of heaven."

> *Let's live for God, continually going forth to win souls for Him.*

Part V

Lessons from Noah and the Ark

A Solemn Message

When God speaks, you and I can afford to listen. It's not man speaking now, but it is God. *Then the LORD said to Noah, Enter the ark, you and all your household* (Genesis 7:1).

Perhaps some sceptic is reading this and says, "I hope Mr. Moody isn't going to teach about the ark. I thought that was given up by all intelligent people."

I haven't given it up. When I do, I am going to give up the whole Bible. There is hardly any portion of the Old Testament Scripture that the Son of God didn't set His seal on when He was here in the world.

Some say, "I don't believe in the story of the flood."

Christ connected His own return to this world with that flood. *For the coming of the Son of Man will be just like the days of Noah. For as in those days before the flood they were eating and drinking, marrying and giving in marriage, until the day that Noah entered the ark, and they did not understand until the flood came and took them all away; so will the coming of the Son of Man be* (Matthew 24:37-39).

I believe the account of the flood just as much as I do the third chapter of John. I pity any man that picks the Word of God to pieces. The moment we give up any one of these things, we give up a piece of the deity of the Son of God. I noticed that when a man begins to pick the Bible to pieces, it doesn't take him long to tear it *all* to pieces. What's the use of taking five years to do what you can do in five minutes?

One hundred and twenty years before God spoke the words in Genesis 7:1, Noah received the most awful communication that ever came from heaven to earth. No man up to that time, and I think no man since, has ever received such a communication. God said that because of the wickedness of the world He was going to destroy the world by water. We can have no idea of the extent and character of that pre-flood wickedness. The Bible piles one expression on another in its effort to emphasize it. *Then the LORD saw that the wickedness of man was great on the earth, and that every intent of the thoughts of his heart was only evil continually. The LORD was sorry that He had made man on the earth, and He was grieved in His heart* (Genesis 6:5-6). *God looked on the earth, and behold, it was corrupt; for all flesh had corrupted their way upon the earth. Then God said to Noah, The end of all flesh has come before Me; for the earth is filled with violence because of them; and behold, I am about to destroy them with the earth* (Genesis 6:12-13). Men lived five hundred years and more then, and they had time to mature in their sins.

How the Message Was Received

For one hundred and twenty years, God strove with the pre-flood civilization. He never destroys without warning, and they had their warning. Every time Noah drove a nail into the ark, it was a warning to them. Every sound of the hammer echoed, "I believe in God." If they had repented and cried as they did at Nineveh, I believe God would have heard their cry and spared them. But there was no cry for mercy. I have no doubt that they ridiculed the idea that God was going to destroy the world. I have no doubt that there were atheists who said there wasn't any God anyhow.

I asked an atheist once, "How do you account for the formation of the world?"

"Oh! force and matter worked together and by chance the world was created."

I said, "It's a remarkable thing that your tongue isn't on the top of your head if force and matter just threw it together in that manner."

If I took out my watch and told you that force and matter worked together and out came the watch, you would say I was a lunatic of the first order, wouldn't you?

And yet they say that this old world was made by chance, and it just threw itself together.

I met a man in Scotland. He took the position that there is no God.

I asked him, "How do you account for the creation of all these rocks?" (They have many rocks in Scotland.)

He said "Why, any school boy could account for that."

"Well, how was the *first* rock made?"

"Out of sand."

"How was the first sand made?"

"Out of rock."

He had it all arranged so nicely. Sand and rock, rock and sand. I have no doubt that Noah had these same type of men to contend with.

Then there are agnostics. They believe there is a God and that the world didn't happen by chance. But they believe God is too merciful and full of compassion to punish sin. The drunkard, the harlot, the gambler, the murderer, the thief, and the man who chases worldly pleasure would all share alike with the saints at the end. Suppose the governor of your state was so tenderhearted that he couldn't bear to have a man suffer, couldn't bear to see a man put in jail, and believed all prisoners should be set free. How long would he be governor? You would have him out of office before the sunset. These very men that talk about God's mercy would be the first to uprise if a governor refused to put a criminal in prison.

Others believe that God couldn't destroy the world even if He wanted to. If a great flood occurred, they would simply retreat to the hills and mountains to escape it. That would be a hundred times better than Noah's ark. Or, if it should come to that, they could build rafts, which would be a good deal better than that ark. They had never seen such an ugly looking thing. It was about five hundred feet long, about eighty feet wide, and fifty feet high. It had three stories and only one small window.

Finally, some believed that Noah must be wrong because he was in such a minority. That is a popular argument now, you know. Noah was greatly in the minority. But he went on working.

Some believed that Noah must be wrong because he was in such a minority.

If they had saloons then, they probably sang vulgar songs about Noah and his ark. I don't doubt that they did, because we read that there was *violence in the land*, and wherever you have alcohol you have violence. We read also that Noah planted a vineyard and fell into the sin of drunkenness. He was a righteous man. If he did that, what must the others have done? And if they had theaters, they likely acted it out to entertain whole families.

If they had the press in those days, reporters would have come to interview him. And the Associated Press would have printed daily updates on how the work on the ark progressed.

And perhaps they had tours where people visited the ark as a spectacle. If Noah happened to be around, they would nudge each other and say, "That's Noah. Don't you think there is a strange look in his eye?"

As a Scotsman would say, they thought him a little foolish. Thank God, a man can afford to be a little insane. An insane man thinks everyone *else* is crazy. A drunkard doesn't call himself insane when he drinks up all his financial resources. But a man is called insane when he gets into the ark and is saved for time and eternity.

All manner of sport was made of Noah and his ark. Businessmen went on buying and selling, and Noah went on preaching and toiling.

They perhaps had some astronomers who gazed up at the stars and said, "Don't be concerned. There's no sign of a coming storm in the heavens. We are very wise men. If there was a storm coming, we could read it in the heavens."

Geologists would continue to dig away and say, "There is no sign in the earth."

Even the carpenters who helped build the ark might have made fun of him. But they were probably like lots of people today who will help build a church, and perhaps give money for its support, but never enter it themselves.

Things went on as usual. Little lambs skipped on the hillsides each spring. Men sought after wealth. If they had leases, I expect they ran for longer periods than ours do. We think ninety-nine years is a long time, but theirs probably ran for nine hundred and ninety-nine years. And when they came to sign a lease, they would say, "Old Noah says the world is coming to an end in one hundred and twenty years, and it's been twenty years. But I guess I'll sign the lease and risk it."

Someone said that Noah must have been deaf, or he could not have stood the mocking and condescending looks from his countrymen. But even if he was deaf to the voice of men, he heard the voice of God clearly when He told him to build the ark.

I can imagine after one hundred years rolled away, and the work on the ark ceased, men said, "Why has he stopped work?"

He went on a preaching tour to tell the people of the coming storm. He warned the people that God was going to sweep every man from the face of the earth unless he took refuge in the ark. But he couldn't get a single man to believe him except his own family.

Some of the old men had passed away. They died saying, "Noah is wrong."

He couldn't get a single man to believe him except his own family.

Poor Noah. He must have had a hard time of it. I don't think I would have had the grace to work for one hundred and twenty years without a convert. But he just toiled on and believed the Word of God.

Then the hundred and twenty years were up. In the spring of that year, Noah didn't plant anything, because he knew the flood was coming. The people said, "Every other year he has planted. This year he thinks the world is going to be destroyed and hasn't planted anything."

Moving In

I can imagine one beautiful morning without a cloud in sight. Noah heard from God. He heard the same voice he heard one hundred and twenty years earlier. Perhaps there had been silence for one hundred and twenty years. But the voice rang through his soul once again: *Noah, come thou and all thy house into the ark* (Genesis 7:1 KJV).

The word *come* occurs about nineteen hundred times in the Bible. This is the first time it meant salvation. It's easy to picture Noah and his family moving into the ark as they carry all their household possessions.

Some of his neighbors probably said, "Noah, what's

your hurry? You'll have plenty of time to get into that old ark. What's your hurry? There are no windows and you can't even look out to see when the storm is coming."

But he heard the voice and obeyed.

Some of his relatives might have said, "What are you going to do with the old homestead?"

Noah possibly said, "I don't want it. The storm is coming. Worldly wealth has no value. The ark is the only place of safety." We must bear in mind that the possessions we think so much of will soon pass away. The heavens will be on fire. Then what will property, honor, and position in society be worth?

The first thing that alarmed them was when they rose one morning, and the heavens were filled with the fowl of the air. They flew into the ark two by two. They came from the desert, the mountains, and all parts of the world. It must have been a strange sight. I can imagine the people cried, "Great God! What's the meaning of this?"

And they looked down on the earth and saw little insects creeping up two by two from all parts of the world. Then came cattle and beasts, two by two. The neighbors cried out, "What does this mean?"

They ran to their statesmen and wise men, who told them there was no sign of a coming storm, and asked them why the birds, animals, and creeping things were drawn toward the ark, as if guided by an unseen hand.

The statesmen and wise men said, "Well, we can't explain it, but don't worry about it. God isn't going to destroy the world. Business has never been better. Do you think God would let us be so prosperous if He was going to destroy the world? There's still no sign of a coming storm. We have no idea what made these insects and wild beasts of the forest go into the ark. We don't understand it. It's very strange. But there's no sign anything is going to happen. The stars are bright, and the sun shines as bright as it ever did. Everything continues on as it always has. You can hear the children playing in the street. Men and women continue to marry."

I imagine the alarm faded, and things returned to normal. Noah came out and said, "The door is going to be shut. Come in. God is going to destroy the world. See how the animals have come? The communication came to them direct from heaven." But the people only continued to mock him.

Do you know, when the hundred and twenty years were up, God gave the world seven days of grace? Did you ever notice that? If there had been repentance during those seven days, I believe it would have been heard. But there was none.

The last day arrived, the last hour, the last minute, and the last second. God Almighty came down and shut the door of the ark. No angel or man, but God Himself shut that door. When the master of the house rose and shut the door, the doom of that old world was forever sealed. The sun had gone down upon the glory of that old world for the last time. From the distance came the mutterings of the storm. The thunder rolled and lightning flashed. The old world reeled. The storm burst upon them. Noah's old ark would have been worth more than the whole world to them.

Some may scoff at this, laugh at the Bible, make fun of your mother's God, or laugh at Christians, but the hour is coming when one promise in the Word of God will be worth more to you than ten thousand worlds like this.

The windows of heaven opened and the fountains of the great deep broke forth. The waters bubbled up, and the sea burst its bounds and leaped over its walls.

God shut that door. When the door was shut, there was no hope.

The rivers swelled. The people in the lowlands fled to the mountains and highlands. They fled up the hillsides. The people wailed, "Noah! Noah! Noah! Let us in!"

They left their homes and came to the ark. They pounded on the ark. They cried, "Noah! Let us in! Noah! Have mercy on us!"

"I'm your nephew!"

"I'm your niece!"

"I'm your uncle!"

A voice cried from inside, "I would like to let you in, but God has shut the door. I can't open it!"

God shut that door. When the door was shut, there was no hope. Their cry for mercy was too late. Their opportunity for grace was over. Their last hour had come. God had pleaded with them and invited them to come in. But they mocked the invitation. They laughed and made fun of the idea of a deluge. Now it was too late.

God didn't permit anyone to survive to tell us how the people perished. When Job lost his family, a messenger came to him. No messenger came from the pre-flood world. Not even Noah himself could see the world perish.

If he could, he would have seen men, women, and children throw themselves against the ark. The waves rose higher and higher, and those outside perished in their unbelief. Some thought to escape by climbing the trees. They thought the storm would end soon. It continued to rain day and night, for forty days and forty nights. They were swept away as the waves dashed against them. The statesmen, astronomers, and great men called out for mercy, but it was too late. They had disobeyed the God of mercy. He had called, and they refused. He had pleaded with them, but they laughed and mocked. The time came for judgment instead of mercy.

Judgment

The time will come again when God deals in judgment with the world. We don't know exactly when, but it is sure to come. God's word has been proclaimed that this world will be rolled up like a scroll and burnt up with fire. What will become of your soul? It is a loving call: *Noah, Come thou and all thy house into the ark* (Genesis 7:1 KJV). Twenty-four hours before the rain began to fall, Noah's ark wasn't worth much more than firewood. But twenty-four hours after the rain began to fall, Noah's ark was worth more than all the world. There wasn't a man still living who wouldn't have given everything for a seat in the ark. You may turn away and laugh.

You may say, "I would rather be without Christ than have Him."

The time is coming when Christ will be worth more to you than ten thousand worlds like this. He is offered to you now. Today is the day of grace. Now is the day of mercy. If you read your Bible carefully, you will find that God always precedes judgment with grace. Grace is a forerunner of judgment. He called the men in the days of Noah in love. They would have been saved if they had repented in those one hundred and twenty years. When Christ came and pleaded with the people in Jerusalem, it was their day of grace. But they mocked and laughed at Him.

He said, *Jerusalem, Jerusalem, who kills the prophets and stones those who are sent to her! How often I wanted to gather your children together, the way a hen gathers her chicks under her wings, and you were unwilling* (Matthew 23:37). Forty years afterward, thousands of the people begged that their lives might be spared. Over one million perished in that city.

In 1857, a revival swept over this country from the east, clear over to the Pacific coast. It was God calling the nation to Himself. Half a million people united with the church at that time. Then the Civil War broke out. The country was baptized with the Holy Spirit in 1857, and in 1861, we were baptized in blood. It was a call of mercy preceding judgment.

Are Your Children Safe?

The Scripture I selected has a special application to Christian people and to parents. This command of the Scripture was given to Noah not only for his own safety but also for that of his household. The question I ask each father and mother is this, "Are your children in the ark of God?" You may brush it off, but it's a very important question. Are all your children in? Are all your grand-children in? Don't rest day or night until you get your children in. I believe my children have fifty temptations where I had one. I believe that in the great cities there is a snare of the Devil on the corner of every street for our sons and daughters. And I don't believe we should squander our time accumulating wealth and worldly possessions. Have I done all I can to get my children in? That's our job. Period.

Now, let me ask another question. How would Noah have felt if, when God called him into the ark, his children refused to go with him? If he had lived such a poor example that his children had no faith in his word, what would he have felt? He would have said, "There's my poor boy on the mountain. I would rather have perished myself."

David cried over his son. *O my son Absalom, my son, my son Absalom! Would I had died instead of you, O Absalom, my son, my son!* (2 Samuel 18:33). Noah loved his children, and they had confidence in him.

Someone sent me a paper a number of years ago. It contained an article that was marked. Its title was "Are all the children in?" An old wife lay dying. She was nearly one hundred years old. The husband who had taken the journey with her, sat by her side. She barely breathed. Suddenly she revived, opened her eyes, and said, "It is so dark."

"Yes, Janet, it's dark."

"Is it night?"

"Yes, it's midnight."

"Are all the children in?"

Her youngest child had been in the grave twenty years.

But she traveled back to the old days that night when she fell asleep in Christ asking, "Are all the children in?"

Are they all in? Ask yourself now. Is John in? Is James in? Or is he immersed in business and pleasure? Is he living a double or dishonest life? Where is your boy, mother? Where is your son and your daughter? Is it well with your children? Can you say it is?

After being superintendent of a Sunday school in Chicago for a number of years – a school of over a thousand members, children that came from godless homes, having mothers and fathers working against me, taking the children off on excursions on Sunday, and doing all they could to break up the work I was trying to do – I used to think that if I should ever stand before an audience, I would speak only to parents. That would be my primary objective. It's an old saying, "Get the lamb, and you will get the sheep." I gave that theory up years ago. Give me the sheep, and then I will have someone to nurse the lamb. If you convert a little lamb, and he has a godless father and mother, you will have little chance with that child. We want godly homes. The home was established long before the church.

That said, I completely disagree with the idea that our children have to grow up before they can be born again. Once, I saw a lady with three daughters at her side. I stepped up to her and asked her if she was a Christian.

"Yes, sir."

Then I asked the oldest daughter if she was a Christian. Her chin quivered, and tears came into her eyes. She said, "I wish I was."

The mother became angry with me and said, "I don't

want you to speak to my children about that. They don't understand." And in a great rage, she stormed off with her daughters in tow. One daughter was fourteen years old, one twelve, and the other ten. Their mother thought they weren't old enough to be talked to about their salvation.

Let them drift into the world and plunge into worldly amusements, and then see how hard it is to reach them. Many sons are now beyond their mother's reach. They will not allow their mothers to pray with them. She may pray *for* them, but they will not let her pray or talk *with* them. When their minds were tender and young, they might have been led to Christ. Bring them in. *Let the children alone, and do not hinder them from coming to Me; for the kingdom of heaven belongs to such as these* (Matthew 19:14). Is there a prayerless father reading this? May God pierce you to your very soul. Make up your mind that, God helping you, you will get your children in. God's order is to the father first, but if he doesn't accept his responsibility, the mother should step in and save the children from the wreck. Now is the time to take the job seriously, while you have them under your roof. Exert your God-given influence over them.

Now is the time to take the job seriously, while you have them under your roof.

I think of two fathers, one lived on the banks of the Mississippi, and the other lived in New York. The first one devoted all his time to amassing wealth. He had a son to whom he was very attached. One day, the boy was brought home badly injured. The father was informed that the boy would only live a short time. He broke the news to his son as gently as possible.

"You say I won't live, Father? Then pray for my soul," said the boy.

That father had never said a prayer for his son, and he told him he couldn't. Shortly after, the boy died. Since then, that father has said that he would give all he possessed if he could call his boy back only to offer one short prayer for him.

The other father had a boy who had been sick for some time. He came home one day and found his wife weeping. She said, "I can't help but believe that this is going to be fatal."

The man said, "If you think so, would you please tell him?"

But the mother couldn't tell her boy. The father went to the sick room and saw that death was close. He said, "My son, do you know you're not going to live?"

The little fellow looked up and said, "No. Is this death I feel coming over me? Will I die today?"

"Yes, my son. You won't live out the day."

The little fellow smiled and said, "Well, Father, I'll be with Jesus tonight, won't I?"

"Yes, you'll spend the night with the Lord." The father broke down and wept.

The little fellow saw the tears and said, "Don't weep for me. I'll go to Jesus and tell Him that ever since I can remember, you have prayed for me."

I have three children. If God chose to take them from me, I would rather have them take that type of a message to Him than to have the wealth of the whole world. I pray to God that I could say something to motivate you, fathers and mothers, to get your children into the ark.

Part VI

Gifts of Grace

Learn from Me, for I am gentle and humble in heart. (Matthew 11:29)

Humility

There is no harder lesson to learn than the lesson of humility. It's not taught in the schools of men, only in the school of Christ. It's the rarest of all the gifts. Very rarely do we find a man or woman who closely follows the footsteps of the Master in meekness and humility. I believe that it's the hardest lesson Jesus Christ taught His disciples while He was here on earth. It almost looked, at first, as though He failed to teach it to the twelve men who had been with Him almost constantly for three years.

I believe that if we are humble enough, we will get a great blessing. And I think that blessing depends more on us than the Lord. He is always ready to give a blessing and give it freely, but we aren't always in a position to receive it. He always blesses the humble. If we can get down in the dust before Him, we won't be disappointed. It was Mary at the feet of Jesus, who had chosen the *good part* (Luke 10:42).

Did you ever notice the reason Christ gave for learning of Him? He could have said, "Learn of me, because I am the most advanced thinker of the age. I have performed miracles that no other man has performed. I have shown my supernatural power in a thousand ways." But no, the reason He gave was that He was *gentle and humble in heart* (Matthew 11:29).

We read of the three men in Scripture whose faces shone. All three were noted for their meekness and humility. We are told that the face of Christ shone at His transfiguration. Moses, after he had been on the mount for forty days, came down from his communion with God with a shining face. And when Stephen stood before the Sanhedrin on the day of his death, his face shone like the face of an angel. If we desire our faces to shine, we must get into the valley of humility and go down in the dust before God.

Bunyan says that it is hard to get down into the valley of humiliation. The descent is steep and rugged. But it is very fruitful, fertile, and beautiful when we get there. I think that no one will dispute that. Almost every man, even the ungodly, admires meekness.

Someone asked Augustine what the most important Christian quality was. He said, "Humility." They asked him what the second was, and he replied, "Humility." They asked him the third, and he said, "Humility." I think that if we are humble, we have all the graces.

Some years ago, I saw what is called a sensitive plant. I happened to breathe on it, and suddenly it drooped its head. I touched it, and it withered away. Humility is as sensitive as that. It can't safely be brought out on exhibition. A man who flatters himself and believes that he is humble and walking close to the Master is self-deceived.

If humility speaks of itself, it is gone.

Humility consists not in thinking poorly of ourselves but in not thinking of ourselves at all. Moses didn't expect his face to shine. If humility speaks of itself, it is gone.

Someone said that the grass is an illustration of this lowly quality. It was created for the lowliest service. Cut it, and it springs up again. The cattle feed upon it, and yet how beautiful it is.

The showers fall upon the mountain peaks, and very often leave them barren, because the water rushes down into the meadows and valleys and makes the lowly places fertile. If a man is proud and lifted up, rivers of grace may flow over him and leave him barren and unfruitful. However, they bring blessing to the man who has been brought low by the grace of God.

A man can imitate love, faith, hope, and all the other graces. But it's very difficult to imitate humility. It's easy to detect fake or imitation humility.

They have a saying in the East, that as the tares and wheat grow, they show which God has blessed. The ears that God has blessed bow their heads and acknowledge every grain. The more fruitful they are, the lower their heads are bowed. The tares which God has sent as a curse, lift their heads erect, high above the wheat, but their only fruit is evil.

I have a pear tree on my farm which is very beautiful. It is one of the prettiest trees on my property. Every branch reaches up to the light and stands almost like a wax candle, but I never get any fruit from it. I have another tree which was so full of fruit last year that the branches almost touched the ground. If we only get down low enough, God will use every one of us to His glory.

As the lark that soars the highest, builds her nest the lowest. As the nightingale that sings so sweetly, sings in the shade when all things rest. As the branches that are most laden with fruit, bend lowest. And as the ship most laden, sinks deepest in the water. Christians who bear the most fruit are the humblest.

Some years ago, *The London Times* told the story of a petition that was being circulated for signatures. It was a time of great excitement, and the petition was intended to have great influence in the House of Lords. But there was one word left out. Instead of reading, "We humbly beseech thee," it read, "We beseech thee." So it was ruled out. If we want to make an appeal to the God of heaven, we must humble ourselves. If we humble ourselves before the Lord, we won't be disappointed.

As I studied the lives of those mentioned in the Bible who demonstrated humility, I grew convicted. I ask you to pray that I may have humility. When I examine my life next to the lives of some of those men, I say, shame on Christianity of the present day. If you want to get a good idea of yourself, look at some of the people in the

Bible that have been clothed with meekness and humility, and note the contrast between their position and your position before God and man.

One of the meekest men in history was John the Baptist. Remember when they asked if he was Elijah, or this prophet, or that prophet?

He said, "No."

He could have said some very flattering things about himself. He could have said, "I am the son of the old priest Zacharias. Haven't you heard of my fame as a preacher? I have probably baptized more people than any man living. The world has never seen a preacher like me."

I honestly believe that *today* most men in his position would do that. Some time ago, I heard a man on the train talking so loud that all the people in the car could hear him. He declared that he had baptized more people than any man in his denomination. He boasted about how many thousands of miles he had traveled, how many sermons he had preached, and how many open-air services he had held. He carried on until I was so ashamed that I hid my head. This is the age of boasting and arrogance. It is the day of the great "I."

I recently realized that in all the Psalms you can't find any place where David refers to his victory over the giant, Goliath. If David lived today, there would have been an entire book written about it immediately. I'm sure many poems would tell of the great things he had done. He would have been in demand as a lecturer, and would have added a title to his name, like G.G.K. for Great Giant Killer. That's how it is today. We have great evangelists, great preachers, great theologians, and great bishops.

"John," they asked, "who are you?"

"I am nobody. I'm to be heard and not seen. I am only a voice."

He didn't have a word to say about himself.

I once heard a little bird faintly singing close by me, but when it got clear out of sight, its notes were even sweeter. The higher it flew, the sweeter its song became. If we can only get self out of sight and learn of Him who is meek and lowly in heart. We will be lifted up into heavenly places.

Mark tells us that John came and preached, *After me One is coming who is mightier than I, and I am not fit to stoop down and untie the thong of His sandals* (Mark 1:7). Think of that. Keep in mind that Christ was looked upon as a deceiver and a village carpenter. Yet here's John, the son of an old priest. John had a much higher position in the sight of men than Jesus. Great crowds came to hear him, and even Herod heard him speak.

When his disciples came and told John that Christ was beginning to draw big crowds, he responded with humility. *John answered and said, A man can receive nothing unless it has been given him from heaven. You yourselves are my witnesses that I said, I am not the Christ, but, I have been sent ahead of Him. He who has the bride is the bridegroom; but the friend of the bridegroom, who stands and hears him, rejoices greatly because of the bridegroom's voice. So this joy of mine has been made full. He must increase, but I must decrease* (John 3:27-30).

It is easy to read that, but hard for us to live in the power of it. It's very hard for us to be ready to decrease, to grow smaller and smaller, so that Christ may increase. The morning star fades away when the sun rises.

> *He who comes from above is above all, he who is of the earth is from the earth and speaks of the earth. He who comes from heaven is above all. What He has seen and heard, of that He testifies; and no one receives His testimony. He who has received His testimony has set his seal to this, that God is true. For He whom God has sent speaks the words of God; for He gives the Spirit without measure.* (John 3:31-34)

Now, let's take a closer look at ourselves. Have we been decreasing? Do we think less of ourselves and of our position than we did a year ago? Are we seeking to obtain some position of dignity? Do we want to hold on to some title, and are we offended because we aren't treated with the respect we think is due us? Some time ago, I heard a man in the pulpit say that he should be offended if he wasn't addressed by his title. Are you going to take that position? Do you believe that you must have a title, and that you must be addressed by that title or be offended? John didn't want *any* title. When we are right with God, we won't care about titles. Early in his ministry, Paul calls himself the *least of the apostles* (1 Corinthians 15:9). Later on he claims to be *the very least of all saints* (Ephesians 3:8). Again, just before his death, he humbly declares that he is the chief of sinners (1 Timothy 1:15). Notice how he seemed to grow smaller and smaller in his own estimation. It was the same with

Do we think less of ourselves and of our position than we did a year ago?

John. I hope and pray that as time passes, we desire to decrease so that He may increase, and let God have all the honor and glory.

Andrew Murray said, "When I look back upon my own religious experience, or round upon the Church of Christ in the world, I stand amazed at the thought of how little humility is sought after as the distinguishing feature of the discipleship of Jesus. In preaching and living, in the daily intercourse of the home and social life, in the more special fellowship with Christians, in the direction and performance of work for Christ. There is an abundance of proof that humility is not esteemed the cardinal virtue, the only root from which the graces can grow, the one indispensable condition of true fellowship with Jesus."

Take a look at what Christ says about John. *He was the lamp that was burning and was shining* (John 5:35). Christ gave him the honor that belonged to him. If you take a humble position, Christ will see it. If you want God to help you, take a low position.

I am afraid that if we had been in John's place, many of us would have said, "What did Christ say? I'm a burning and shining light?" Then we would have had that acknowledgement put in the newspaper and had copies sent to our friends with that part highlighted. Sometimes I receive an envelope just full of clippings from the newspapers, from a man stating how eloquent he is. The whole point is that the man wants me to get him a church. Do you think that a man who has such eloquence would be looking for a church? No, they would all be looking for him.

Isn't that embarrassing? Sometimes I think it's a wonder

that any man is converted these days. Let others praise you. Don't praise yourself. If we want God to lift us up, let us get down. The lower we get, the higher God will lift us. It is Christ's eulogy of John: *Among those born of women there has not arisen anyone greater than John the Baptist* (Matthew 11:11).

There is a story told of William Carey, the great missionary, that he was invited by the governor-general of India to go to a dinner party. In attendance were some military officers who belonged to the aristocracy and who looked down on missionaries with scorn and contempt.

One of those officers said at the table, "I believe Carey was a shoemaker, wasn't he, before he took up the profession of missionary?"

Mr. Carey spoke up and said, "Oh no, I was only a cobbler. I could only mend shoes." He wasn't ashamed of it.

The one prominent virtue of Christ, next to His obedience, is His humility. And even His obedience grew out of His humility. *Although He existed in the form of God, did not regard equality with God a thing to be grasped, but emptied Himself, taking the form of a bond-servant, and being made in the likeness of men. Being found in appearance as a man, He humbled Himself by becoming obedient to the point of death, even death on a cross* (Philippians 2:6-8). In His lowly birth, His submission to His earthly parents, His seclusion during thirty years, His consorting with the poor and despised, His entire submission and dependence upon His Father, this virtue that was consummated in His death on the cross, shines out.

One day, Jesus was on His way to Capernaum and talked about His coming death, suffering, and about His resurrection. He heard quite a heated discussion going on behind Him. When He came into the house at Capernaum, He turned to His disciples and said, "What was all that discussion about?"

I can picture John looking at James, and Peter at Andrew, and they all looked ashamed. "Who shall be the greater?" That discussion has wrecked party after party, one society after another.

To teach them humility, Christ placed a little child in their midst and said, *Whoever receives this child in My name receives Me, and whoever receives Me receives Him who sent Me; for the one who is least among all of you, this is the one who is great* (Luke 9:48).

To me, one of the saddest things in the life of Jesus Christ was the fact that just before His crucifixion, His disciples argued about who should be the greatest. That same night He instituted the Last Supper, and they ate the Passover together. It was His last night on earth. They never saw Him as sorrowful before. He knew Judas was going to sell Him for thirty pieces of silver and that Peter would deny Him. And in addition to that, when going into the very shadow of the cross, there arose this strife about who should be the greatest. He took a towel and girded Himself like a slave. Then He took a basin of water, stooped down, and washed their feet. That was another object lesson of humility. *You call Me Teacher and Lord; and you are right, for so I am. If I then, the Lord and the*

Teacher, washed your feet, you also ought to wash one another's feet (John 13:13-14).

When the Holy Spirit came, those men were filled. That moment in time marked the difference. Matthew took up his pen to write, and he kept himself out of sight. He tells what Peter and Andrew did, but he calls himself "the publican." He tells how they left everything to follow Christ, but doesn't mention the feast he gave.

> *I wish I had the same spirit, that I could just get out of sight and hide myself.*

Jerome says that Mark's gospel is to be considered Peter's memoirs and to have been published by his authority. Yet in it we constantly find that damaging things are mentioned about Peter, and things to his credit are not referred to. Mark's gospel omits all reference to Peter's faith in venturing on the sea, but goes into detail about the story of his fall and denial of our Lord. Peter put himself down and lifted others up.

If the gospel of Luke was written today, it would be signed by the great Dr. Luke, and his picture would be on the cover. But you can't even find Luke's name in that gospel. He keeps himself out of sight. He wrote two books, and his name isn't found in either.

John hid himself under the expression "the disciple whom Jesus loved." None of the four men whom history credits as the authors of the Gospels, lay claim to their authorship in their writings. I wish I had the same spirit, that I could just get out of sight and hide myself.

I believe our only hope is to be filled with the Spirit of Christ. My prayer is that God will fill us with meekness and humility. Let's embrace the hymn, "O, To Be Nothing, Nothing," and make it the language of our hearts. It breathes the spirit of Him who said, *The Son can do nothing of Himself* (John 5:19).

> Oh, to be nothing, nothing!
> Only to lie at His feet,
> A broken and emptied vessel—
> For the Master's use made meet!
> Emptied that He might fill me
> As forth to His service I go;
> Broken, that so unhindered
> His life through me might flow.

A gentleman came to me once and asked which promise of Christ's I thought was the most precious. I took some time to look them over, but gave up. I found that I couldn't answer his question. It's like a man with a large family of children. He can't tell someone which child he likes best, because he loves them all. But even if it's not the best, this is one of the sweetest promises of all. *Come to Me, all who are weary and heavy-laden, and I will give you rest. Take My yoke upon you and learn from Me, for I am gentle and humble in heart, and you will find rest for your souls. For My yoke is easy and My burden is light* (Matthew 11:28-30).

There are many people who think the promises are not going to be fulfilled. There are some we already see fulfilled and can't help but believe they're true. It's important to remember that all the promises are not given without conditions. Some are given with, and others without, conditions attached to them. For instance, it says, *If I regard wickedness in my heart, the LORD will not hear* (Psalm 66:18). I don't even need to worry about prayer as long as I'm cherishing some known sin. He will not hear me, much less answer me.

For the LORD God is a sun and shield; The LORD gives grace and glory; No good thing does He withhold from those who walk uprightly (Psalm 84:11). I have no claims under that promise unless I walk uprightly.

Some of the promises were made to certain individuals or nations. For instance, God promised that He would make Abraham's seed to multiply as the stars of heaven. That's not a promise for you or me. Some promises were made to the Jews and don't apply to the Gentiles.

Then there are promises without conditions. He promised Adam and Eve that He would send a Savior. There was no power that could keep Christ from coming at the appointed time. When Christ left the world, He promised to send us the Holy Spirit. He had only been gone ten days when the Holy Spirit came. So you can run right through Scripture, and you will find that some of the promises are with, and some without, conditions. And if we don't comply with the conditions, we can't expect them to be fulfilled.

In the end, I believe that everyone on the face of the earth will be compelled to testify that if they complied with the conditions, the Lord fulfilled the Scriptures to the letter. Joshua, the old Hebrew hero, serves as an illustration. He tested God for forty years in the Egyptian brick kilns, forty years in the desert, and thirty years in the Promised Land. With all that, his dying testimony was that *not one word of all the good words which the LORD your God spoke concerning you has failed; all have been fulfilled for you, not one of them has failed* (Joshua 23:14). I believe it would be easier to lift the ocean than to break one of God's promises. So when we come to a promise like the one we're looking at now, we cannot easily dismiss it. *Come to Me, all who are weary and heavy-laden, and I will give you rest* (Matthew 11:28).

You might think there's nothing new to learn from this familiar passage. When I pick up a photo album, I don't care if the photos are new but rather if I know the faces. It's the same with these old, well-known texts. They have quenched our thirst before, but the water is still bubbling up and it's impossible to drink it dry.

The cry of the world today is, "Where can rest be found?"

If you probe the human heart, you'll find a want. That want is rest. The cry of the world today is, "Where can rest be found?" Society spends a lot of time, energy, and money in establishments of amusement. What's the draw of Sunday driving, bars, and restaurants? Some people think they're pursuing these things for pleasure, others think they are going to find it in wealth, and others in literature. They earnestly seek rest but don't find it.

Where Can Rest Be Found?

If I wanted to find a person who had rest, I wouldn't go among the very wealthy. The man that we read of in the twelfth chapter of Luke thought he was going to get rest by multiplying his goods, but he was disappointed. *And I will say to my soul, Soul, you have many goods laid up for many years to come; take your ease, eat, drink and be merry* (Luke 12:19). I venture to say that there is not a person in this wide world who has tried to find rest in that way and found it.

Money can't buy it. Many millionaires would gladly pay millions if they could purchase it like stocks and shares. God made the soul a little too large for this world. We could possess the entire world and a void would still exist. There is a lot involved in getting wealth, and even more in keeping it.

Nor would I seek rest among the pleasure seekers. They indulge in a few hours of enjoyment one day. Then the next day, there's enough sorrow to counterbalance it. They can drink the cup of pleasure today, but the cup of pain comes on tomorrow.

To find rest I would *never* go among the politicians, or among the so-called great. Congress is the last place on earth I would go. In the Lower House they want to go to the Senate. In the Senate they want to go to the Cabinet. Then they want to go to the White House. Rest has never been found *there*.

Nor would I go among the halls of learning. *Excessive devotion to books is wearying to the body* (Ecclesiastes 12:12). I wouldn't go among high society, because they're constantly chasing after fashion. Have you ever noticed their troubled faces out in public? And the face is a window to the soul. They have no hopeful look. Their worship of pleasure is slavery. Solomon tried pleasure and found bitter disappointment. In the end came the bitter cry, *All is vanity* (Ecclesiastes 1:2).

There is no rest in sin. The wicked know nothing about it. The Scriptures tell us *But the wicked are like the tossing sea, for it cannot be quiet, and its waters toss up refuse and mud* (Isaiah 57:20). Perhaps you've been on the sea when there is a calm. The water is crystal clear, and it seems as if the sea is at rest. But if you looked closely you would see the current, and that the calm is only on the surface. Man, like the sea, has no rest. He has had no rest since Adam fell. And there will be none for him until he returns to God again, and the light of Christ shines into his heart.

Rest cannot be found in the world, and thank God, the world can't take it from the believing heart. Sin is the cause of all the unrest. It brought toil, labor, and misery into the world.

Now for something positive. For someone who has heard the sweet voice of Jesus, and laid his burden down at the cross, there is rest, sweet rest. Thousands could testify to this blessed fact. They could say truthfully:

> I heard the voice of Jesus say,
> "Come unto me and rest;
> Lay down, thou weary one, lay down
> Thy head upon my breast."
> I came to Jesus as I was,
> Weary, and worn, and sad.
> I found in Him a resting-place,
> And He hath made me glad.[3]

Among all his writings, Saint Augustine has nothing

---

3   Excerpt from a hymn titled "I Heard the Voice of Jesus Say"

sweeter to say than this: "Thou hast made us for Thyself, O God, and our heart is restless till it rests in Thee."

Do you know that for four thousand years no prophet, priest, or patriarch ever stood up and spoke like this? It would have been blasphemy for Moses to have uttered those words. Do you think he had rest when he displeased the Lord? Do you think Elijah could have uttered such a text as this when he prayed that he might die under the juniper tree?

This is one of the strongest proofs that Jesus Christ was not only man, but also God. He was God-man, and this is heaven's proclamation: *Come to me, ... and I will give you rest.* He brought it down from heaven with Him.

Now, if this text wasn't true, don't you think we would have found out by this time? I believe it as much as I believe in my own existence. Why? Because I not only find it in the Word of God, but also in my own experience. The promises of Christ have never been broken, and never can be.

I thank God for the word *give* in that passage. He doesn't sell it. Some of us are so poor that we couldn't buy it if it was for sale. Thank God, we can get it for nothing.

I like to have a text like this, because it is relevant to all of us. *Come to Me, all who are weary and heavy-laden.* That doesn't mean a select few refined ladies and cultured men. It doesn't mean good people only. It applies to saint and sinner. Hospitals are for the sick, not for healthy people. Christ wouldn't shut the door in anyone's face and say, "I didn't mean *all*. I only meant certain ones." If you can't come as a saint, come as a sinner. Only come.

A lady told me once that she was so hard-hearted she couldn't come.

"Well," I said, "it doesn't say all ye softhearted people come. Black hearts, vile hearts, hard hearts, soft hearts, all hearts come. Who can soften your hard heart but Him?"

The harder the heart, the more you need to come. If my watch stops, I don't take it to a drug store or to a blacksmith's shop. I take it to the watchmaker to have it repaired. So if the heart gets out of order, take it to its keeper, Christ, to have it set right. If you can prove that you're a sinner, you're entitled to the promise. Get all the benefit you can out of it.

There are many believers who think this text applies only to sinners. It's just the thing for them too. What do we see today? The church, Christian people, all loaded down with cares and troubles. *Come to Me, all who are weary and heavy-laden.* All! I believe that includes the Christian whose heart is burdened with some great sorrow. The Lord wants you to come.

Christ the Burden-Bearer

Therefore humble yourselves under the mighty hand of God, that He may exalt you at the proper time, casting all your anxiety on Him, because He cares for you (1 Peter 5:6-7). The church would stand victorious if Christian people realized that. But they never made that discovery. They agree that Christ is the sin-bearer, but they don't realize that He is also the burden-bearer. *Surely He hath borne our griefs and carried our sorrows* (Isaiah 53:4 KJV). It is the privilege of every child of God to walk in unclouded sunlight.

Some people go back into the past and rake up all their troubles. Then they look into the future and anticipate that they will have still more trouble. They go reeling and staggering all through life.

We want to eradicate this long-faced Christianity from the face of the earth.

They give you the cold chills every time you interact with them. They put on a whining voice and tell you what a hard time they've had. I believe they carry their troubles in their back pocket and bring them out at every opportunity.

The Lord says, "Cast all your cares on Me. I want to carry your burdens and your troubles." What we want is a joyful church, and we're not going to convert the world until we have it. We want to eradicate this long-faced Christianity from the face of the earth.

Take the people that bring some great burden into a meeting. If you can keep their attention, they will say, "Oh, wasn't it grand! I forgot all my cares." That's because they dropped their bundle at the end of the pew. But the moment the benediction is pronounced, they grab the bundle again. You laugh, but you do it yourself. Cast your cares on Him.

Sometimes these people go into their closet and close the door. They get so carried away and lifted up that they forget their trouble, but they just pick it up again the moment they get off their knees. Leave your sorrow now. Cast all your cares upon Him. If you can't come to Christ as a saint, come as a sinner. But if you're a saint with some trouble or care, bring it to Him. Saint and sinner, come. He wants you all. Don't let Satan deceive you into believing that you can't come if you're willing. Christ says, *And you are unwilling to come to Me* (John 5:40).

A man in one of our meetings in Europe said he would like to come, but he was chained and couldn't come.

A Scotsman said to him, "Ay, man, why don't you come chain and all?"

He said, "I never thought of that."

Are you angry and easily irritated? Do you make things unpleasant at home? Come to Christ, and ask Him to help you. Whatever your sin is, bring it to Him.

What Does It Mean to Come?

You say, "Mr. Moody, I wish you'd tell us what it means to come." I've given up trying to explain it. I always feel like people look at me like I'm speaking a foreign language.

The way to heaven is the way of the cross. Don't try to get around it.

The best definition is just – come. The more you try to explain it, the more people are confused. About the first thing a mother teaches her child is to look. She takes the baby to the window and says, "Look, Papa is coming!"

Then she teaches the child to come. She props the baby up against a chair and says, "Come!" Sure enough, the little thing pushes the chair along towards mamma. That's coming. You don't need to go to college to learn how. You don't need any minister to tell you what it is. Will you come to Christ? He said, *The one who comes to Me I will certainly not cast out* (John 6:37).

When we have such a promise as this, let's cling to it and never give it up. Christ is not mocking us. He wants us to come with all our sins and backslidings, and throw ourselves into His loving arms. God doesn't just want our tears. He wants our sins. Tears alone do no good. And we cannot come through willpower. Action is necessary. How many times at church have we said, "I will turn over a new leaf." But the Monday leaf is worse than the Saturday leaf.

The way to heaven is the way of the cross. Don't try to get around it. Do you know what the *yoke* referred to in the Matthew 11 text is? It's the cross which Christians must bear. The only way you can find rest in this dark world is by taking up the yoke of Christ. I don't know what that may include in your case, beyond accepting your Christian duties, acknowledging Christ, and behaving like one of His disciples. Perhaps it may be to erect a family altar, tell a godless husband that you've made up your mind to serve God, or tell your parents that you want to be a Christian. Follow the will of God, and happiness, peace, and rest will come. The way of obedience is always the way of blessing.

I preached in Chicago to a hall full of women one Sunday afternoon. After the meeting was over, a lady came to me and said she wanted to accept Christ. After some conversation she went home. I looked for her for a whole week, but didn't see her until the following Sunday afternoon. She came and sat down right in front of me, and looked like she had lost her best friend. She seemed to have entered into misery instead of the joy of the Lord.

After the meeting was over, I went to her and asked what the trouble was.

She said, "Oh, Mr. Moody, this has been the most miserable week of my life."

I asked her if there was anyone she had trouble with and whom she couldn't forgive.

She said, "No, not that I know of."

"Well, did you tell your friends about having found the Savior?"

"Indeed I didn't. I've been trying to keep it from them all week."

"Well," I said, "that's the reason you have no peace."

She wanted to take the crown, but didn't want the cross. My friends, you must go by the way of Calvary. If you ever get rest, you must get it at the foot of the cross.

She said, "If I go home and tell my unbelieving husband that I found Christ, I don't know what he'll do. I think he will kick me out."

I said, "If that happens, leave."

She left and promised she would tell him. She visibly looked timid and pale, but she didn't want another wretched week. She was determined to have peace.

The next night I gave a lecture to men only. In the hall, there were eight thousand men and one solitary woman. When I finished and transitioned into the question-and-answer time, I found this lady with her husband. She introduced him to me. He was a doctor and a very influential man.

She said, "He wants to become a Christian."

I took my Bible and told him all about Christ, and he

accepted Him. I said to her after it was all over, "It turned out quite differently from what you expected, didn't it?"

"Yes," she replied. "I was never so scared in my life. I expected he would do something horrible, but it turned out so well."

She took God's way and got rest.

I want to say to young ladies, perhaps you have a godless father or mother or a skeptical brother who is destroying his life with alcohol. Perhaps there is no one who can reach them but you. Many times a godly, pure, young lady has taken the light into some dark home. Many homes could be lit up with the gospel if the mothers and daughters would only speak the Word.

The last time Mr. Sankey and I were in Edinburgh, a father, two sisters, and a brother sat every morning, read my sermon in the paper, and picked it to pieces. They were furious to think that the Edinburgh people should be inspired by such preaching. One day, one of the sisters was going by the hall. She thought she would drop in and see what class of people went there.

She happened to take a seat by a godly lady who said to her, "I hope you're interested in this work."

She tossed her head and said, "I am absolutely not. I'm disgusted with everything I've seen and heard."

"Well," said the lady, "perhaps you came with a pre-conceived expectation."

"Yes, and the meeting has not removed any of it, but reinforced it."

"I have received a great deal of good from them."

"There is nothing here for me. I don't see how an intellectual person can be interested."

To make a long story short, the godly lady got her to promise to come back. When the meeting broke up, just a little of the preconception had worn away. She promised to come back again the next day and then attended three or four more meetings. She became quite interested. She said nothing to her family until the burden became too heavy. Then she told them. They laughed at her and made her the butt of their jokes.

One day the two sisters were together and the other said, "Now what do you have from those meetings that you didn't already have?"

"I have a peace that I never knew before. I am at peace with God, myself, and all the world." She continued, "I have self-control. If you said half the mean things before I was converted that you've said since, I would have been angry and answered back. But if you remember correctly, I haven't answered once since I've been converted."

The sister said, "You certainly have something that I don't have." The converted sister told her it was for her too. She brought her sister to the meetings, and she found peace.

Like Martha and Mary, they had a brother, but he was a member of the University of Edinburgh. Could it be possible for him to be saved? To go to the meetings? It might be okay for *women*, but not for him. One night they came home and told him that a friend of his from the university had stood up and confessed Christ. When he sat down, his brother got up and confessed. Finally, the last brother stood up and confessed.

When the young man heard it, he said, "Do you mean to tell me that he has been converted?"

"Yes."

"Well," he said, "there must be something to it."

He put on his hat and coat, and went to see his friend Black. Black brought him down to the meetings, and he was converted.

Isn't it time for us to get our friends into the kingdom of God?

We proceeded to Glasgow, and had not been there six weeks when news came that that young man had become ill and died. When he was dying, he called his father to his bedside and said, "Wasn't it a good thing that my sisters went to those meetings? Won't you meet me in heaven, Father?"

"Yes, my son. I'm so glad you are a Christian. That's the only comfort I have in losing you. I will become a Christian and will see you again."

My intention is to encourage some sister to go home and carry the message of salvation. None of us are guaranteed tomorrow. It may be that your brother will be taken away from you in a few months. We are living in solemn days. Isn't it time for us to get our friends into the kingdom of God? Come, wife, won't you tell your husband? Come, sister, won't you tell your brother? Won't you take up your cross now? The blessing of God will rest on your soul if you will.

I was in Wales once, and a lady told me this little story. An English friend of hers, a mother, had a daughter that was sick. At first, they thought there was no danger. Then one day the doctor came in and said the symptoms were very serious. He took the mother out of the room and told her that the child would not live. It came like a thunderbolt. After the doctor left, the mother went into the room where her daughter lay and talked to the child and tried to divert her mind.

"Darling, do you know you will soon hear the music of heaven? You will hear a sweeter song than you have ever heard on earth. You will hear them sing the song of Moses and the Lamb. You are very fond of music. Won't it be sweet, darling?"

The little, tired, sick child turned her head away and said, "Oh Mamma, I'm so tired and so sick that I think it would make me worse to hear all that music."

"Well," the mother said, "you will soon see Jesus. You will see the seraphim and cherubim and the streets all paved with gold." She went on picturing heaven as it's described in Revelation.

The little child again turned her head away and said, "Oh Mamma, I'm so tired that I think it would make me worse to see all those beautiful things."

At last, the mother took the child up in her arms and pressed her to her loving heart. The little one whispered, "Oh Mamma, that's what I want. If Jesus will only take me in His arms and let me rest."

Aren't you tired and weary of sin? Aren't you weary of the turmoil of life? You can find rest in the arms of the Son of God.

Part VII

I Will

Seven *I Wills* of Christ

When a man says, "I will," it may not mean much. We very often say, "I will," when we have no intention of doing what we say. But when Christ says, *I will,* He intends to keep His word. Everything He promised to do, He is able and willing to accomplish. And He's going to do it. I can't find any passage in Scripture where He tells us He will do something, then leaves it undone. He always does what He says.

Salvation

The first *I will* we're going to look at, is found in John's gospel. *The one who comes to Me I will certainly not cast out* (John 6:37).

I imagine someone will say, "Well, if I was what I should be, I would come. But when I think about my past, it's too dark. I am not fit to come."

You must bear in mind that Jesus Christ didn't come to save the upright and the just. He came to save sinners like you and me, who have gone astray, sinned, and come short of the glory of God. Listen to this *I will*. It goes right into the heart. *The one who comes to Me I will certainly not cast out.* Surely that is broad enough, isn't it? I don't care who the man or woman is. I don't care what their trials, troubles, sorrows, or sins are. If they will only come straight to the Master, He will not cast them out. Come then, poor sinner. Come just as you are and take Him at His word.

You must bear in mind that Jesus Christ didn't come to save the upright and the just.

He is so anxious to save sinners. He will take everyone who comes. He will take those who are so full of sin that they are despised by all who know them. He will take those who have been rejected by their parents and have been left by their wives. He will take those who have sunk so low that others don't even look upon them with pity any longer. His occupation is to hear and save. That's what He left heaven and came into the world for. He left the throne of God to save sinners. *For the Son of Man has come to seek and to save that which was lost* (Luke 19:10). *For God did not send the Son into the world to judge the world, but that the world might be saved through Him* (John 3:17).

A wild and wasteful young man, who was running headlong into ruin, came into one of our meetings in Chicago. The Spirit of God got hold of him. While I talked with him and attempted to bring him to Christ, I quoted that verse to him.

I asked him, "Do you believe Christ said that?"

"I suppose He did."

"Suppose He did! Do you believe it?"

"I hope so."

"Hope so! Do you believe it? You do your work, and the Lord will do His. Just come as you are, and throw yourself into His arms. He will not cast you out."

The young man thought it was too simple and easy.

At last, light seemed to break in upon him, and he seemed to find comfort from it. It was past midnight when he got down on his knees, but down he went. He was converted.

I said, "Now, don't think you're going to get out of the Devil's territory without trouble. The Devil will come to you tomorrow morning and say it was all emotion, and you only imagined you were accepted by God. When he does, don't fight him with your own opinions. Fight him with John 6:37. *All that the Father gives Me will come to Me, and the one who comes to Me I will certainly not cast out.*"

I don't believe that any man even starts to come to Christ before the Devil attempts to somehow trip him up. And even after he has come to Christ, the Devil tries to attack him with doubt and make him believe he isn't really saved.

The struggle came sooner than I thought in this man's case. When he was on his way home, the Devil attacked him. He used this text, but the Devil put this thought into his mind: *How do you know Christ ever really said that? Perhaps the translators made a mistake.*

Into the darkness he went again. He was in trouble till about two in the morning. At last, he came to this conclusion. He said, "I will believe it anyway. And when I get to heaven, if it isn't true, I'll just tell the Lord *I* didn't make the mistake – the translators did."

When the kings and princes of this world issue invitations, they invite the rich, the mighty, the powerful, the honorable, and the wise. But the Lord, when He was on earth, called around Him the vilest of the vile. That was the principal fault the people found with Him. Those self-righteous Pharisees weren't going to associate with harlots and publicans. The principal charge against Him was that *this man receives sinners and eats with them* (Luke 15:2). John Bunyan would not have been socially desirable in his time. He, a Bedford tinker, couldn't get inside one of the princely castles. I was very much amused when I was overseas. They had erected a monument to John Bunyan, and it was unveiled by lords, dukes, and other great men. While he was on earth, they wouldn't have allowed him inside the walls of their castles. Yet, he was made one of the mightiest instruments in the spread of the gospel. No book that has ever been written comes as close to the Bible as John Bunyan's *Pilgrim's Progress*. And he was a poor Bedford tinker. That's how it is with God. He picks up some poor, lost outcast and makes him an instrument to turn hundreds and thousands to Christ.

George Whitefield, standing in his tabernacle in London with a multitude gathered around him, cried out, "The Lord Jesus will save the Devil's castaways!"

Two poor, abandoned women outside in the street heard him as his silvery voice rang out into the air. Looking into each other's faces, they said, "That must mean you and me." They wept and rejoiced. They approached the building and looked inside. The earnest messenger had tears streaming from his eyes as he pleaded with the people to give their hearts to God. One of the women wrote him a little note and sent it to him.

Later that day, as he sat at the table of Lady Huntingdon, who was his special friend, someone present said, "Mr. Whitefield, didn't you go a little too far today when you said that the Lord would save the Devil's castaways?"

He took the note from his pocket and gave it to the lady. He said, "Will you read that note aloud?"

She read, "Mr. Whitefield, two poor lost women stood outside your tabernacle today. We heard you say that the Lord would save the Devil's castaways and seized upon that as our last hope. We write you this to tell you that we rejoice now in believing in Him. From this good hour we shall endeavor to serve Him who has done so much for us."

Cleansing

The next *I will* is found in Luke. We read of a leper who came to Christ. *While He was in one of the cities, behold, there was a man covered with leprosy; and when he saw Jesus, he fell on his face and implored Him, saying, Lord, if You are willing, You can make me clean. And He stretched out His hand and touched him, saying, I am willing; be cleansed. And immediately the leprosy left him* (Luke 5:12-13). If any man or woman full of the leprosy of sin reads this, go to the Master and tell all your case to Him. He will speak to you as He did to that poor leper and say, *I am willing; be cleansed*. The leprosy of your sins will flee away from you. It is the Lord, and the Lord alone, who can forgive sins. If you say to Him, "Lord, I am full of sin. *You can't make me clean*. Lord, I have a terrible temper. *You can't make me clean*. Lord, I have a deceitful heart. Cleanse me, O Lord. Give me a new heart. Give me the power to overcome the flesh and the snares of the Devil. Lord, I'm full of unclean habits."

If you come to Him with a sincere spirit, you will hear His voice: *I am willing; be cleansed*. It will be done. Do you think that if the God who created the world out of nothing, says, "Thou shalt be clean," you will somehow not be clean?

You can make a wonderful exchange today. You can have health in the place of sickness, and you can get rid of everything that is vile and hateful in the sight of God. The Son of God comes down and says, "I will take away your leprosy and give you health instead. I will take away that terrible disease that is ruining your body and soul, and give you my righteousness instead. I will clothe you with the garments of salvation."

Isn't that wonderful? That's what He means when He says, *I will*. Oh, grab hold of this *I will*.

Confession

Therefore everyone who confesses Me before men, I will also confess him before My Father who is in heaven (Matthew 10:32). There's the *I will* of confession.

That's the next thing that takes place after a man is saved. When we have been washed in the blood of the

Lamb, the next thing is to open our mouths. We have to confess Christ here in this dark world, and tell others about His love. We are not to be ashamed of the Son of God.

A man thinks it's a great honor when he has achieved something that causes his name to be mentioned in the English Parliament, or in the presence of the Queen and her court. How excited we used to be during the war when some general did something extraordinary, and someone got up in Congress to proclaim his exploits. In China, we read, the highest ambition of a successful soldier is to have his name written in the palace or temple of Confucius. Just think of having your name mentioned in the kingdom of heaven by the Prince of Glory, by the Son of God, because you confess Him here on earth. If you confess Him here, He will confess you there.

If you wish to be brought into the clear light of liberty, you must take your stand on Christ's side.

If you wish to be brought into the clear light of liberty, you must take your stand on Christ's side. I have known many Christians who grope around in the darkness and never get into the clear light of the kingdom, because they were ashamed to confess the Son of God. We are living in a day when men want a religion without the cross. They want the crown but not the cross. But if we are to be disciples of Jesus Christ, we must take up our crosses, not once a year or on the Sabbath, but daily. And if we take up our crosses and follow Him, we will be blessed in the very act.

I remember a man in New York who used to come and pray with me. He had his cross. He was afraid to confess Christ. He kept his Bible hidden in the bottom of his drawer. He wanted to get it out and read it to his roommate but was ashamed to do it. For a whole week that was his cross. After he carried the burden that long and after a terrible struggle, he made up his mind. *I will take my Bible out tonight and read it.* He took it out. Soon he heard the footsteps of his roommate coming upstairs.

His first impulse was to put it away again, but he decided not to. He would face his companion with it. His mate came in, saw him with his Bible, and said, "John, are you interested in these things?"

"Yes," he replied.

"For how long?" asked his companion.

"Exactly a week," he answered. "For a whole week I've tried to get my Bible out to read to you, but I've never done so till now."

"Well," said his friend, "it's a strange thing. I was converted on the same night, and I too was ashamed to take my Bible out."

You are ashamed to take your Bible out and say, "I have lived a godless life for all these years, but from now on I will live a life of righteousness." You are ashamed to open your Bible and read that blessed psalm: *The LORD is my shepherd; I shall not want* (Psalm 23:1). You are ashamed to be seen on your knees. No man can be a disciple of Jesus Christ without bearing His cross. A great many people want to know how it is that Jesus Christ has so few disciples, while Muhammad has so many. The reason is that Muhammad requires no cross to bear. There are so few Christians who will come out and take their stand.

I was struck during the American war with the fact that there were so many men who could go to the cannon's mouth without trembling, but who didn't have the courage to pick up their Bibles to read them at night. They were ashamed of the gospel of Jesus Christ, which is the power of God unto salvation. *Therefore everyone who confesses Me before men, I will also confess him before My Father who is in heaven. But whoever denies Me before men, I will also deny him before My Father who is in heaven* (Matthew 10:32-33).

Service

The next *I will* is of service.

Many Christians get excited and feel compelled to say, "I want to do some service for Christ."

Well, Christ says, *Follow me, and I will make you fishers of men* (Matthew 4:19).

All Christians can help to bring someone to the Savior. Christ says, *And I, if I am lifted up from the earth, will draw all men to Myself* (John 12:32). Our job is just to lift up Christ.

Our Lord said, *Follow me, and I will make you fishers of men.* They simply obeyed Him. Then on the day of Pentecost, we see the result. Peter had a good haul that day. I doubt he ever caught as many fish in one day as he did men on that day. It would have broken every net they had on board if they had to drag up three thousand fish.

I read some time ago of a man who took passage in a stagecoach. There were first-, second-, and third-class passengers. But when he looked into the coach, he saw all the passengers sitting together without distinction. He didn't understand it till they came to a hill.

The coach stopped, and the driver called out, "First-class passengers keep their seats. Second-class passengers get out and walk. Third-class passengers get behind and push."

In the church, we have no room for first-class passengers who think that salvation means an easy ride all the way to heaven. We have no room for second-class passengers who are carried most of the time, and when they must work out their own salvation, they trudge along and never give a thought to

In the church, we have no room for first-class passengers who think that salvation means an easy ride all the way to heaven.

helping their brothers and sisters. All church members ought to be third-class passengers. We should all be ready to dismount and push all together, and push with a will. That was John Wesley's definition of a church, "All at it, and always at it."

Every Christian ought to be a worker. He doesn't need to be a preacher or an evangelist to be useful. He may be useful in business. An employer can be used by God as he labors with his employees and within his realm of business relations. Often a man can be far more useful in a business sphere than he could in another.

There is one big reason why so many don't succeed. I have been asked by many good men, "Why is it we don't have any results? We work hard, pray hard, and preach hard. Yet success doesn't come." I'll tell you why. It is because they spend all their time mending their nets. No wonder they never catch anything.

It's critical to hold inquiry meetings, and pull the net in to see if you've caught anything. If you are always mending and setting the net, you won't catch many fish. Who ever heard of a man going out to fish, setting his net, letting it stop there, and never pulling it in? Everybody would laugh at the man's foolishness.

A minister in England came to me one day and said, "I wish you'd tell me why we ministers don't succeed better than we do."

I explained the idea of pulling in the net and said, "You ought to pull in your nets. There are many ministers in Manchester who can preach much better than I can, but I pull in the net."

Many people have objections to inquiry meetings, but I impressed upon him the importance of them. The minister said, "I've never pulled in my net, but I'll try next Sunday."

He did so, and eight persons, anxious inquirers, joined him in his study to have their questions about salvation answered. The next Sunday he came to see me and said he had never had such a Sunday in his life. He came face to face with a marvelous blessing. The next time he drew the net, forty inquired about the gospel. When he came to see me later, he said to me, "Moody, I've had eight hundred conversions this last year! It was such a huge mistake that I didn't begin to pull in the net earlier."

If you want to catch men, just pull in the net. If you only catch one, it will be something. It may be a little child, but I've known a little child to convert a whole family. You don't know what's in that little boy in the inquiry room. He may become another Martin Luther, a reformer who will make the world tremble. You can never tell. God uses the weak things of this world to confound the mighty. God's promise is as good as a bank note. And here is one of Christ's promissory notes: *Follow me, and I will make you fishers of men.* Will you grab hold of the promise, trust it, and follow Him now?

If a man preaches the gospel, and preaches it faithfully, he ought to expect results then and there. I believe it is the privilege of God's children to reap the fruit of their labor 365 days a year.

Some say, "Isn't there a time for sowing as well as harvesting?"

Yes, it's true, there is. But you can sow with one hand and reap with the other. What would you think of a farmer who went on sowing all year round and never thought of reaping? Again, we want to sow with one hand and reap with the other. If we look for the fruit of our labors, we will see it. *And I, if I am lifted up from the earth, will draw all men to Myself.* We must lift Christ up, seek men out, and bring them to Him.

You must use the right kind of bait. Many don't do this and wonder why they're not successful. You see them try different types of entertainment to try and catch men. This is a step in the wrong direction. This perishing world wants Christ, and Him crucified. There's a void inside every man that wants to be filled up. If we approach them with the right kind of bait, we will catch them. This dying world needs a Savior. If we are going to be successful in catching men, we must preach Christ crucified. We must preach not only His life but also His death. If we are faithful in doing this, we will succeed. And why? Because of His promise. *Follow me, and I will make you fishers of men.* That promise is just as valid to you and me as it was to His disciples. It is as true now as it was in their time.

Think of Paul up yonder. People are going home to be with the Lord every day and every hour, men and women who have been brought to Christ through his writings. He set streams in motion that have flowed on for more than a thousand years.

I can imagine men going up there and saying, "Paul, thank you for writing that letter to the Ephesians. I found Christ in that."

"Paul, I thank you for writing that epistle to the Corinthians."

"Paul, I found Christ in that epistle to the Philippians."

"I thank you, Paul, for that epistle to the Galatians. I found Christ in that."

I suppose they go up to Paul all the time and thank him for what he did. When Paul was put in prison he didn't fold his hands and sit in idleness. No, he wrote. And his epistles have come down through the ages of time. They have brought thousands upon thousands to a knowledge of Christ crucified. Yes, Christ said to Paul, "I will make you a fisher of men if you will follow Me." And he has been fishing for souls ever since. The Devil thought he had done a very smart thing when he maneuvered Paul into prison. He was very much mistaken. He overdid it for once. I have no doubt that Paul has thanked God ever since for that Philippian jail, his stripes, and imprisonment there. We will only know when we get to heaven what an impact Paul had on the world.

Comfort

The next *I will* is found in John's gospel. *I will not leave you as orphans; I will come to you* (John 14:18).

To me it's a sweet thought that Christ hasn't left us alone in this dark wilderness here below. Although He has gone up on high and taken His seat by the Father's throne, He has not left us alone. He didn't leave Joseph when they cast him into prison. God was with him. When Daniel was cast into the den of lions, they put the Almighty in with him. They were so bound together that they could not be separated. So God went down into the den of lions with Daniel.

If we've got Christ with us, we can do all things. Let's not be focused on how weak we are. Let's lift our eyes up to Him and think of Him as our Elder Brother, who has all power given to Him in heaven and on earth. He says, *And lo, I am with you always, even to the end of the age* (Matthew 28:20). Some of our children and friends leave us, and it's a very sad hour. But, thank God, the believer and Christ will never be separated. He's with us here, and we'll be with Him in person for eternity. Not only is He with us, but He also sent us the Holy Spirit. Let's honor the Holy Spirit

Let's honor the Holy Spirit by acknowledging that He's here in our midst.

by acknowledging that He's here in our midst. He has power to give sight to the blind, liberty to the captive, and to open the ears of the deaf that they may hear the glorious words of the gospel.

Resurrection

Then there is another *I will* in the sixth chapter of John. It occurs four times in that chapter alone. *I Myself will raise him up on the last day* (John 6:40).

I rejoice to think that I have a Savior who has power over death. My blessed Master holds the keys of hades and of death. I received more comfort out of that promise than anything else in the Bible. It brought me joy and lit up my path.

Some time ago, a dear brother died. And as I went into the room and looked upon the lovely face of that brother, that passage ran through my soul. My brother will rise again. I said, "Thank God for that promise." It was worth more than the world to me.

When we laid him in the grave, it seemed as if I could hear the voice of Jesus Christ saying, "Thy brother shall rise again." Blessed promise of the resurrection.

Glory

Father, I desire that they also, whom You have given Me, be with Me where I am. (John 17:24)

This was in the context of His last prayer in the guest chamber, on the last night before He was crucified and died that terrible death on Calvary. Many believers light up at the thought that they will see the King in His beauty in heaven. There is a glorious day before us in the future. Some think that on the first day we're converted we've got everything. To be sure, we get salvation for the past and peace for the present. But then there's still the glory for the future in store. That's what kept Paul rejoicing. He considered his afflictions, his stripes, and his stonings as nothing, compared to the glory that was to come. He considered those things nothing, so that he could win Christ. So when things go against us, let's cheer up. Remember that the night will soon pass away, and the morning will dawn upon us. Death never comes there. It's banished from that heavenly land. Sickness, pain, and sorrow are not permitted entrance to mar that grand and glorious home where we will live forever with the Master. God's family will be all together there. It's a glorious future, my friends! And it may be a great deal nearer than many of us think. During these few days we have here on earth, let us stand steadfast and firm. In eternity we will dwell in the world of light, and the King will reign in our midst.

About the Author

Dwight L. Moody, determined to make a fortune, arrived in Chicago and started selling shoes. But Christ found him and his energies were redirected into full-time ministry. And what a ministry it was. Today, Moody's name still graces a church, a mission, a college, and more. Moody loved God and men, and the power of a love like that impacts generations.

Often disguised as something that would help him, evil accompanies Christian on his journey to the Celestial City. As you walk with him, you'll begin to identify today's many religious pitfalls. These are presented by men such as Pliable, who turns back at the Slough of Despond; and Ignorance, who believes he's a true follower of Christ when he's really only trusting in himself. Each character represented in this allegory is intentionally and profoundly accurate in its depiction of what we see all around us, and unfortunately, what we too often see in ourselves. But while Christian is injured and nearly killed, he eventually prevails to the end. So can you.

The best part of this book is the Bible verses added to the text. The original Pilgrim's Progress listed the Bible verse references, but the verses themselves are so impactful when tied to the scenes in this allegory, that they are now included within the text of this book. The text is tweaked just enough to make it readable today, for the young and the old. Youngsters in particular will be drawn to the original illustrations included in this wonderful classic.

Available where books are sold.